D1570401

Ascending
Jacob's Ladder

Ascending Jacob's Ladder

JEWISH VIEWS OF ANGELS, DEMONS, AND EVIL SPIRITS

Ronald H. Isaacs

JASON ARONSON INC.
Northvale, New Jersey
Jerusalem

This book was set in 12 pt. Garamond Book by Yankee Typesetters, Inc.

Library of Congress Cataloging-in-Publication Data
Isaacs, Ronald H.
    Ascending Jacob's ladder : Jewish views of angels, demons, and evil spirits
    / Ronald H. Isaacs.
        p.   cm.
    Includes bibliographical references and index.
    ISBN 0-7657-5965-9 (alk. paper)
    1. Angels (Judaism)   2. Demonology, Jewish.   I. Title.
BM645.A6183   1997
296.3′15 — dc21   96-39813

Manufactured in the United States of America. Jason Aronson Inc. offers books and cassettes. For information and catalog write to Jason Aronson Inc., 230 Livingston Street, Northvale, NJ 07647.

For my daughter
Keren Lital,
an angelic ray of sunshine.

CONTENTS

INTRODUCTION

Do you believe in Angels? If so, how do they appear to you? George Gallup's polling firm found that 75 percent of 13 to 18-years-olds do. That was back in 1988. Probably more do now.

The winged wonders of the Bible and religious lore are more popular than ever, turning up everywhere from paper dolls to comic books. There are angel newspapers, angel toys, angel calendars, comic books, songbooks, ornaments, and more than 200 books on angels. Angels play a part in such literary classics as John Milton's *Paradise Lost* and the mythology of many other faiths, including Judaism, Christianity, and Islam, all of which accept the existence of angels in varying degrees. In the past few years there has been a markedly increased attempt on the part of these religions to infuse their adherents with a religious passion that seeks to find the true meaning of life itself. In Judaism in particular, the longing for religious passion, mysticism and spiritual connectedness once found only in more orthodox and esoteric forms of Judaism (most notably in Hasidism) has now begun to manifest itself in other streams of Judaism as well. This type of Jewish renewal is giving an ancient religion a whole new spirit, resulting in boosted

interest in a variety of spiritual concerns and ideas. One of
the ever-continuing areas of growing interest is that of
angelology, specifically Jewish angels, the so-called messengers of God.

There are more than 300 references to angels in the
Bible, including angels who often presage special events to
herald God's presence, ministering angels, and soldier
angels directly linked to miraculous events. Although
angels have permeated Jewish tradition beginning with Bible times and later appeared in a plethora of rabbinic writings including the Talmud, Zohar, and the prayerbook,
there is relatively little known about them. At best they
continue to remain a mystery, even though more and more
people are declaring their belief in their existence.

This volume intends to introduce readers to the world of
angels from earliest times to the modern period. It will
include sections on angels in the Bible, Talmud, Midrash,
liturgy, Jewish philosophy, mysticism, and chasidic lore.
Other entries in the book include a section on the classi-
fication of angels, angels in the Apocrypha, good and fallen
angels, angels among ancient Jewish sects, the role of Satan,
demons and evil spirits, angel quotations from a variety of
sources, and a who's who angel glossary.

May this book stimulate your thinking regarding the role
of angels in Jewish tradition, as well as the role that they
may still play in your own personal life. Three thousand
years ago, the psalmist (Ps. 103:20–21) addressed the
angels as follows: "Bless God, all you angels, you mighty in
strength, who do God's bidding and obey God's word.
Bless, God, all you hosts . . ." May you too be blessed in
God's name and may your angels serve as your inspira-
tional guardians.

Ronald H. Isaacs

1

ANGELS IN THE BIBLE

There are a myriad of references to angels in the Bible. They appear in a variety of forms, sometimes as humans and sometimes in other shapes, such as cherubim, the first type of angel that will be examined. They can speak, sit, stand, walk, be clothed, have weapons, ride horses, and decend from heaven on a ladder. Their functions include worshipping God, singing God's praises, acting as go-betweens, announcing forthcoming events, guarding various places, transmitting revelations to prophets and carrying out divine messages. Because of this latter function the Hebrew name "malach"—messenger—has been given to these beings. The Greek translation of "malach" is "angelos," from which the word "angel" is derived. Belief in angels was widespread in the ancient Near East. The gods of the Mesopotamians and Hittites had their subordinate messengers, as did the Egyptian gods who also had divine couriers. Undoubtedly the concepts of these Near Eastern societies worked to form the background out of which biblical stories of angels emerged. Our exploration of angels will begin in the Book of Genesis, with the first reference to a specific kind of angel called a "cherub," appearing in the story of the Garden of Eden.

Cherubim

The Bible frequently refers to "cherubim"—a type of celestial being—to be distinguished from "cherubs," those adorable, chubby, winged infants with rosy cheeks that fly around in Western art. The etymology of the Hebrew word for cherub, "keruv," has been subject to different interpretations. The Tur Sinai, a Bible commentator, explained that the word "keruv" was derived from the Aramaic "karov," meaning "to plow," which is based on Ezekiel's substitution of the face of a cherub (10:14) for that of an ox (1:10) whose main function is to plow. Others have commented that the word "keruv" is derived from the Akkadian "karabu," meaning "to pray or to bless." Thus a cherub served as an intermediary who brought the prayers of humans to the gods. Figures of winged creatures were well known in the art of the ancient Near East, appearing on pottery incense altars from Megiddo as well as flanking the throne of Hiram, king of Byblos. In the Bible, cherubim appear for the first time as guardians of the garden of Eden after Adam and Eve were expelled: "To the east of the garden of Eden God placed the cherubim" (Gen. 3:24). The purpose of these beings was to guard the way to the tree of life.

In the desert tabernacle, hammered golden cherubim faced each other on the cover of the Ark of the Covenant (Exod. 25:18–22; 37:7–9). They are described as facing one another on the two ends of the covering above the Ark of the Covenant, forming the throne of God with their outstretched wings. They are the counterparts of two very large cherubim found in the Holy of Holies of King Solomon's Temple. The allusion to this specific role of the cherubim is found in biblical passages where God is spoken of as "the one who sits enthroned upon the cherubim" (1

Sam. 4:4, 1 Kings, 19:15). Cherubim were also worked into the woven tapestry of the inner curtain and veil in front of the Holy of Holies, the inner sanctum of the Temple (Ex. 26:1,31; 36:8,35).

In one of the most spectacular and amazing visions of all of the Jewish prophets, Ezekiel, in the first chapter of his book, describes each of four cherubim as having four wings and four faces (1:6). Two of their wings spread out above touch one another, and the other two cover their bodies. Their four faces include that of a man, a lion on the right side, an ox on the left side and an eagle (Ezek. 1:10). Under their wings on their four sides they are described as possessing human hands, while each of their feet are like a calf's foot, sparkling like burnished bronze (Ezek. 1:7–8).

Figures of the cherubim were also used for decorative purposes. In Exodus 26:31, they are described as having been embroidered on the veil separating the holy place from the most Holy, on the tabernacle curtains (Ex. 26:1), and carved both on the inner and outer walls and the doors of the inner and outer sanctuary (1 Kings 6:29, 32,35).

The only references in the Talmud to cherubim are "aggadic" or so-called legendary ones. In the tractate of Sukkah 5b, the word "cherub" is interpreted to mean "like a child," derived from the Aramaic "rabia" which means "a child." This interpretation may have influenced Renaissance art, which often pictured the cherub as a winged child.

The talmudic *tractate of Yoma 21a* lists the cherub among the five things which were in the first Jerusalem Temple but not in the Second Temple.

The talmudic *tractate of Baba Batra 99a* has a fairly lengthy debate related to the physical positioning of the cherubim in the Holy of Holies. Whereas Rabbi Yochanan stated that they face each other, Rabbi Eleazar stated that their faces are inward. The Talmud explains further that since the cherubim represented the relationship of love between God and His people, when Israel failed to fulfill God's Will the cherubim were turned toward one another, whereas when Israel fulfilled God's will they not only were facing each other, but they were intertwined in a love embrace.

Of the four-faced variety of cherubim appearing in the Book of Ezekiel, *the Peskita de-Rabbi Eliezer 4* explains as follows: "When God spoke facing the east the voice came from between the two cherubs with human faces, and when God spoke facing the south the voice emerged from between the two cherubs having the face of a lion."

The *Midrash Rabbah* (*Num. 4:13*) states that the position of the terrestrial Sanctuary corresponded to that of the heavenly Sanctuary, and the position of the Ark of the Covenant corresponded to God's heavenly throne. Above the Ark was a cover upon which were two cherubim, symbolizing heaven and earth. The seat of God (i.e. God's heavenly throne) was between them, as it is written: "One cherub at the one end, and one cherub at the other end" (Ex. 25:19).

The question of how images such as cherubim could have had a place in the Israelite cult which is generally imageless has not been satisfactorily answered. It has been conjectured that the cherubim belonged to an old mythological tradition that was unable to be dislodged, and hiding them away in a place such as the Holy of Holies minimized their accessibility and thus the danger of worshipping them. In any event, by the time of the destruction of the First Temple (586 B.C.E.) they disappeared and were not reconstructed when the Second Temple was built.

Hagar's Angels

Hagar, the Egyptian maidservant of Sarah, appears in several early stories in the Book of Genesis. When she conceived, she became contemptuous of Sarah, who in turn abused her until she fled into the wilderness. There, by a spring, Hagar encountered an angel who exhorted her to return, giving her a favorable oracle concerning her future son who would become known as Ishmael:

> An angel of God found her by a spring of water in the wilderness and spoke: "Hagar, slave of Sarah, from whence have you come and where are you going?" And Hagar answered, "I am running away from my mistress Sarai." And the angel of God said to her, "Return to your mistress and submit to her cruel treatment. I will greatly increase your offspring. . . . Behold, you are with child and shall bear a son. His name shall be called Ishmael, for God has paid attention to your suffering. [Gen. 16:7–11]

In this passage, the angel of God appeared as a comforter to the pregnant Hagar, helping to assuage her pain in time of great difficulty. In the following second story, Hagar, after giving birth to Ishmael, was banished along with her son by an exceedingly jealous and outraged Sarah. Once again, Hagar encountered an angel:

> . . . Hagar burst into tears. God heard the cry of the boy and an angel of God called to Hagar from heaven and said to her, "What is bothering you, Hagar? Do not be afraid, for God has heard the cry of the boy where he is. Come and lift up the boy and hold him by the hand, for I will make a great nation of him." Then God

opened her eyes and she saw a well of water. She went and filled the skin with water, and let the boy drink. [Gen. 21:16–19]

In this encounter as well as the previous one, there was nothing supernatural performed by God's angel. On each occasion the angel (which goes unnamed) offered a despondent Hagar hope, comfort and trust in the future. It should also be noted that Hagar's angel, as well as many of the other angels in the Bible, appeared in human form, so that the individuals to whom they appeared were at first quite unaware of their angelic natures.

The Binding of Isaac

Few narratives have been subjected to as much comment and study as the binding of Isaac. In this tale of suspense and intrigue, Abraham is called upon by God to travel to a yet unannounced place and sacrifice his beloved son Isaac. It is an obvious attempt to test Abraham's faith. In a dream-like sacrifice, Abraham ascends Mount Moriah, places his son Isaac on the altar and picks up the knife. The story then continues:

Then an angel of God called to him from heaven: "Abraham, Abraham . . . Do not lift your hand against the boy . . . For now I am convinced that you fear God, since you have not withheld your son, your favorite son, from Me" [Genesis 22:11–12].
And the angel of God called to Abraham a second time out of heaven, and said: "By Myself have I sworn, says God, because you have done this thing and have not withheld your son, your only son. That in blessing I will bless you, and in multiplying I will mul-

tiply your seed as the stars of the heaven . . ."[Gen. 22:15–17]

In this story, the angel of God is strictly God's messenger, disavowing the human sacrifice of Isaac. Again, there is nothing miraculous that is performed by God's angels. Abraham, rather than the angel, found a ram in the thicket of brush which he used as a substitute sacrifice for his son Isaac. The message of the angel established the important message that unlike in paganism, human sacrifice is unacceptable.

Additionally, Abraham learned from the angel's second calling of the divine favor that had been promised to him, which included the proliferation of his descendants. The voice of this angel helped to pave the way for Abraham's status as the first patriarch of the Israelites.

Gateway to Heaven: Angels and Jacob's Ladder

Jacob's ladder is the first explicitly recorded dream in the Bible. Ostensibly to find a wife from among his own kinsmen, but actually trying to escape the wrath of his twin brother Esau, Jacob set out for the land from whence his mother had come. Since travel after sunset became out of the question, Jacob lay down to spend the night under the open sky. There, on the road from Beersheba to Haran, he experienced an extraordinary dream vision that was eventually to prove a turning point in his life:

> He had a dream; a ladder was set on the ground and its top reached to the sky, and angels of God were going up and down on it. And God was standing beside him and God said, "I am Adonai, the God of your father Abraham and the God of Isaac. The ground on which you are lying I will give to you and your off-

spring . . . Remember, I am with you and I will protect you wherever you go and will bring you back to
this land. I will not leave you until I have done what I
have promised you." Jacob awoke from his sleep and
said, "Surely God is in this place, and I did not know
it." Awestruck, he said, "How awesome is this place.
This is none other than the abode of God, and that is
the gateway to heaven." [Gen. 28:12–17]

In this his first encounter with God, fear and trembling is
produced. Unlike in pagan mythology in which stairways
often become passages of communication between humans and the gods, Jacob's ladder does not serve this purpose. God does not descend the ladder nor does Jacob
ascend it in an attempt to reach the divine realm. The
ladder appears to be for the angels alone, whose purpose
seems to be purely ornamental, rather than playing a role
in Jacob's "vision" of God.

Commentators have viewed the angels of God with different interpretations. For instance, the Midrash Tanchuma
holds that the angels were the princes of the heathen nations which God showed to Jacob. Jacob's dream thus depicted the rise and fall of nations and their cultures on the
arena of world history. Thus, according to the Midrash, the
dream of Jacob was not understood as the dream of Jacob
the individual, but rather of Jacob as the symbol of Israel.
The angels symbolized the embodiment of the wanderings
of the Jewish people, as they were exiled from one country
to another, witnessing the rise and fall of mighty kingdoms
such as Egypt, Assyria and Babylon.

Rashi, the great medieval commentator, was comfort-
able with the plain sense of the narrative and believed that
the episode dealt with Jacob the individual. His concern,
however, was with the phrase "ascending and descending"
in reference to the angels. Surely, Rashi queried, the angels

of God should have first descended from the heavens, and then ascended. Rashi answers that the angels that accompanied Jacob in the Holy Land do not go outside the Holy Land. They therefore ascended to Heaven, whereas the angels outside of the Holy Land descended in order to accompany him. This was another way of saying that Jacob needed different guardians on foreign land from those that protected him in his own birthplace. But, wherever Jacob went, God saw fit to equip him with guardian angels!

Finally, the rabbis of *Midrash Rabbah* (*Gen. 28:12*) related the entire Jacob episode of the ladder and the angels to the Mount Sinai experience. The ladder represented Mount Sinai, the angels of God alluded to Moses and Aaron. It is most interesting that in *gematriah* both the Hebrew word for ladder ("sulam") and the Hebrew word for Sinai ("seenai") have the same numerical value of 130!

In this story of Jacob's ladder, the angels did not speak a single word to the sleeping Jacob. Rather, God was the prime speaker, and this theophany with the accompaniment of angels convinced Jacob that this place where he dreamed and slept was an abode of God. Perhaps the angels and the ladder pointing to the heavens provided Jacob with the hope and confidence for inheriting the covenant while affording him some comfort from the pain of the crisis with his brother Esau. In commemoration of this realization, Jacob built an altar in the area and renamed the place Bethel, "the House of God."

Wrestling With an Angel

It had been some twenty years since Jacob had seen his brother Esau, having deceived him out of his birthright. As Jacob now approached his homeland, the fear of his brother Esau revived in him. Jacob knew well that his brother might still wreak vengeance upon him and his family.

As Jacob rose up that night, he first sent his two wives, his two handmaidens and his eleven children over the Jabbok River, a tributary of the Jordan. Left alone, he was about to experience a crisis in his own personal spiritual history:

> Jacob was left alone. And there wrestled a man with him until the breaking of the day. And when he saw that he was unable to prevail, he touched the hollow of his thigh. And the hollow of his thigh was strained. And he said, "Let me go, for the day breaks." And he said, "I will not let you go, unless you bless me." And he said to him "What is your name?" And he answered: "Jacob." And he said: "Your name shall no more be called Jacob, but Israel, for you have striven with God and with men, and have prevailed." And Jacob asked, "Tell me I pray, what is your name." And he answered, "Wherefore is it that you ask after my name?" And he blessed him there. And Jacob called the name of the place Peniel, for "I have seen God face to face, and my life is preserved." [Gen. 32:25–31]

Since ancient times, crossing a river has been symbolic of overcoming peril and going forward to a new experience. In this sense, Jacob passing over the Jabbok to meet Esau crossed the watershed of his life. In order for him to reconcile with his brother Esau, he had to become a different person.

Ancient near Eastern tradition held that rivers were infested by demons. Thus, some have argued that the "man" whom Jacob met that fateful night was some type of river demon. The request by the adversary that Jacob let him go before the breaking of dawn serves to fortify the belief that

Jacob indeed had encountered a demonic being. For the one who could hold on to a demon long enough could bend him to his will.

Many other interpretations of this unknown adversary have emerged over the centuries. Rabbi Samuel ben Nachman in the *Midrash Rabbah* (*Gen. 38:1*) identifies Jacob's adversary as either the angel Michael or Gabriel. These angels are identified in early rabbinic literature as guardian angels who permanently serve God. The Rashbam, a medieval commentator, was of the opinion that since Jacob wished to flee from Esau, God sent the angel from whom he would not flee, so that he might see the fulfillment of God's promise that Esau would do him no harm. Rashi, the great Bible commentator, was of the opinion that the unknown adversary was "the prince of Esau—the spiritual power of Esau." This would help us to understand why this particular place and hour was chosen for the fight. Before Jacob actually encountered Esau in the flesh, his spirit struggled with that of Esau's. Only after the prince of Esau acknowledged his title to the paternal blessing was Jacob, injured and limping, able to go forth to meet his brother Esau and become reconciled with him.

Nahum Sarna, in his commentary on the Book of Genesis saw in the mysterious being the celestial patron of Esau. This is also the interpretation given in the *Midrash, Genesis Rabbah* 77:2. Throughout the ancient world, the idea was current that each people and each city state had its own divine protector. Thus the assailant in the story of Jacob and the mysterious adversary has been understood to be none other than the celestial patron of Esau-Edom, who is the habitual enemy of the Israelite people.

Still other commentators held that Jacob was fighting with his own conscience, eventually emerging from the fight and the dark side of himself purified in soul and in spirit.

Whoever the adversary was, it certainly was no ordinary being. Jacob himself attests to this fact when he says (Gen. 32:31) in naming the site of the encounter "Peniel:" "I have seen a divine being face to face." Centuries later the prophet Hosea (12:4–5), whose words were chosen as part of the Haftarah that accompanies the Bible reading that incorporates this story, refers to this same incident and describes Jacob as having striven with "divine beings," "an angel." Jacob's angel had no definable personality. It was nameless and without character, vanishing as suddenly as it had appeared. However, there can be no doubt as to the far-reaching implications of the encounter. Jacob had passed the test of fitness and did not falter when wrestling with the assailant. He was changed as a person and his name changed from Jacob, meaning "a follower," to Israel—"champion of God." This passage thus represents the spiritual maturation of Jacob. He met with a heavenly being, prevailed, received the blessing of the heavenly being that wrestled with him and received the consequent name change from Jacob to Israel. From this point on, the names Jacob and Israel are used interchangeably for the patriarch, and for the Jewish people who descend from his twelve sons. The Jews also eventually become known as "B'nai Yisrael"—children of Israel.

The Burning Bush Angel

Along with God, it is the figure of Moses who dominates most of the Bible. Born during Jewish enslavement in Egypt, Moses experienced the wondrous and commanding presence of God while tending the flock of Jethro, his father-in-law:

Now Moses, tending the flock of his father-in-law Jethro, the priest of Midian, drove the flock into the desert, and came to Horeb, the mountain of God. An angel of God appeared to him in a blazing fire out of a bush. He gazed, and there was the bush all aglow, and yet the bush was not consumed. Moses said, "I must turn aside to look at the wondrous sight; why does the bush not burn up?" When God saw that he had turned aside to look, God called to him out of the bush: "Moses, Moses." He answered, "Here am I." And God said, "Do not come closer. Remove your sandals from your feet, for the place on which you are standing is holy ground. I am," God said, "the God of your father, the God of Abraham, the God of Isaac and the God of Jacob." And Moses hid his face, for he was afraid to look at God. And God continued, "I have marked well the plight of My people in Egypt and have listened to their cry because of their taskmasters . . . Come therefore, I will send you to Pharaoh, and you shall free My people, the Israelites, from Egypt." [Ex. 3:1–6, 10]

This story provides us with the first theophany (i.e. revelation of God) to Moses. He first saw an angel of God which appeared out of a burning bush that is eternally aglow with flames. It was only after Moses realized that this was a special bush that God directly spoke to him.

In this story, the angel who appeared to Moses acted as God's messenger, getting his attention which prepared him to hear of his mission. Bachya ibn Pakuda, a Spanish commentator who lived during the latter half of the eleventh century, explained the necessity of the gradual process of ascent by which Moses ultimately perceived the Divine Presence. This, he believed, was necessary, since Moses was only a novice when it came to experiencing prophecy. Bachya stated that first Moses saw the fire that took hold of the bush which was not consumed, and then desired to get a closer look in order to determine whether it was the bush or fire that was unusual. After he saw the fire, his perception of God's angel grew stronger. Finally, as his inner perception of the angel grew stronger, Moses experienced a prophetic vision, the glory of the Divine Presence. Rabbi Joshua ben Karcha held a similar opinion as stated in the *Midrash Rabbah* (*Ex. 2, 5*), in which he stated that the angel appeared first to Moses, acting as an intermediary and standing in the center of the fire, and afterwards the Shechinah (i.e. Divine Presence) descended and spoke with Moses from the midst of the thorn bush. In this explanation, the angel was sent by God to help set Moses at ease and prepare him for his first audience with God.

Rabbi Yochanan, in the *Midrash Rabbah* (*Ex. 2:5*) went so far as to identify the angel of God as Michael, whereas Rabbi Chanina identified the angel as Gabriel. Both Michael and Gabriel appear for the first time by name in the Book of Daniel (Michael in Daniel 10:21 and Gabriel in Daniel 8:16). As we shall later see, these are two of four angels who are described in rabbinic legend as both visiting Abraham after his circumcision and surrounding the throne of the Almighty.

Balaam's Angel

In the Balaam story we see the most memorable and almost miraculous episode of the first animal, a talking donkey, which was able to perceive an angel of God. Alongside the serpent that tempted Eve, the most famous animal in the Bible is the pagan prophet Balaam's talking donkey. The episode dates back to Balak, the King of Moab, who

had persuaded his messenger Balaam to come to his terri-
tory and put a curse upon the Israelites. En route his donkey sees the angel:

> And Balaam rose up in the morning, and saddled his
> donkey, and went with the princes of Moab. And
> God's anger was kindled because he went and the
> angel of God was kindled because he went. And the
> angel of God placed himself in the way of the adver-
> sary against him . . . And the donkey saw the angel
> of God standing in the way, with his sword drawn in
> his hand, and the ass turned aside out of the way, and
> went into the field. And Balaam smote the ass, to turn
> her into the way. Then the angel of God stood in a
> hollow way between the vineyards, a fence being on
> this side, and a fence on that side. And the donkey saw
> the angel of God, and she thrust herself into the wall,
> and crushed Balaam's foot against the wall, and he
> smote her again. And the angel of God went further,
> and stood in a narrow place, where there was no way
> to turn either right or left. And the donkey saw the
> angel of God, and she lay down under Balaam and
> Balaam's anger was aroused and he smote the donkey
> with his staff. And God opened the mouth of the don-
> key and she said to Balaam: "What have I done to you,
> that you have hit me these three times?" And Balaam
> said to the donkey: "Because you have mocked me, I
> would there were a sword in my hand, for now I had
> killed you." And the donkey said to Balaam: "Am I not
> your donkey, upon which you have ridden all your
> life? Have I been in the habit of doing this to you?" And
> he answered, "No". Then God uncovered Balaam's
> eyes, and he saw the angel of God standing in the way,
> his sword drawn in his hand. Thereupon he bowed
> right down to the ground. The angel of God then said

to him, "Why have you hit your donkey three times? It is I who came out as an adversary, for the errand is obnoxious to me. When the donkey saw me, she shied away because of me those three times. If she had not shied away from me, you are the one I should have killed, while sparing her." Balaam then said to the angel of God, "I made a mistake because I did not know that you were standing in my way. If you still disapprove, I will turn back." But the angel of God said to Balaam, "Go with the men. But you will say only that which I will tell you." [Num. 23:21–35]

In this story, filled with subtle humor and sarcasm, Balaam the pagan prophet prepared himself to curse the Israelites. Even God viewed his intent with alarm, since curses among the ancient Israelites were considered a method of translating a harmful effect into a reality. Both traditional Jewish and Christian interpretation have viewed the speech of the donkey to be a miracle, designated to magnify and glorify God's name, God having given the donkey the capability of human speech. The main burden of this biblical tale is not the speaking of the donkey but the ability of the donkey to see the angel, contrasted to the evil Balaam who looks and yet is blind. Over and against both of them stands God, who is in control of both.

According to the *Midrash Rabbah* (*Numbers 20:13–14*), the sword-bearing angel of God was an angel of mercy, but to Balaam he made himself an adversary. Maimonides, the medieval philosopher and rationalist, understood the entire scene to be a prophetic vision.

Clearly the angel in this story acted as God's messenger, forcing both the donkey and ultimately its rider Balaam to submit to the power of the Divine. The angel always acted as God's agent and never initiated any action on its own. No magic rites could prevail over the Supreme Master.

Balaam had no choice but to utter the words that God had put into his mouth.

Toward the end of the story, now able to see what his eyes were unable to see at the beginning of his mission, Balaam pronounced one blessing after another. As he stood on a hilltop overlooking the Israelite tents having had his eyes opened by the angel, God's spirit now took hold of Balaam, and out of his mouth came this beautiful description of the Israelite camp: "How fair are your tents, O Jacob, your dwellings O Israel" (Num. 24:5).

Rabbinic interpretation has seen in this verse the ideal of the Jew in his home and synagogue, and for this reason it was placed as the opening prayer at the beginning of the daily morning service. It expresses the feelings of joy and reverence on entering a synagogue, the House of God.

Joshua's Angel

The children of Israel finally reached the Promised Land after a forty-year trek in the wilderness. Moses had learned earlier from God that he would be denied entrance, and died with the privilege of seeing the land of milk and honey from afar. No sooner than did his successor, Joshua, take over as commander-in-chief of the Israelites, that the first vision of an angel disguised as a man occurred to him:

> Once, when Joshua was near Jericho, he looked up and saw a man standing before him, with a sword drawn in his hand. Joshua approached him and asked, "Are you one of us or one of our enemies?" He replied, "No, I am captain of God's host. Now I have come." Joshua threw himself face down to the ground and prostrating himself, said to him, "What does my lord command his servant?" The captain of God's host

answered Joshua, "Remove your sandals from your feet, for the place on which you are standing is holy." And Joshua did so. [Josh. 5:13–15]

In this early episode in the life of Joshua, he was visited by an angel in the form of a man. God sent the angel (with a sword in hand symbolizing victory) to encourage Joshua upon his impending invasion of Jericho. Joshua appeared unaware of the ethereal character of his visitor, taking him for a soldier. Once Joshua realized that he was speaking to the captain of God's army, he fell to his face and bowed. The demand of the angel to have Joshua remove his sandals is most reminiscent of that of Moses at the burning bush who was also told to remove his sandals as a mark of reverence.

This passage has been explored by many commentators. Rashi, the medieval commentator, identified the angel in the story as none other than the archangel Michael. Gershon ben Levi, also known as Gersonides or the RaLBaG, a thirteenth-century philosophical, biblical commentator, understood the passage as a dream in which Joshua visualized himself actually standing with the walls of Jericho. He shared Maimonides's belief that it is impossible to perceive an angel except in an prophetic vision. The fifteenth-century commentator Abrabanel, however, maintained that an angel who assumes a human form can be perceived in a conscious state.

One thing that is clear from this story is that the angel bore the word of God who sent him, acting solely as God's messenger. Unlike Moses, who in the story of the burning bush dealt first with an angel and then directly with God, Joshua did not deal directly with God. Although he patterned his response after Moses by taking off his shoes, he was not being presented as another Moses.

Gideon's Angel

Gideon, an Israelite judge, was known for his decisive victory over the Midianites, constant oppressors of the Israelites. After defeating them decisively, he was offered the kingship but refused out of loyalty to the principle that God is King of Israel (Judg. 6–8). Prior to this battle, Gideon had the following encounter with an angel:

And the angel of God came and sat under the terebinth which was in Ophrah, that belonged to Joash the Abiezrite. His son Gideon was beating out wheat in the winepress, to hide it from the Midianites. And the angel of God appeared to him, and said: "God is with you, you mighty man of valor." And Gideon said: "Oh, my lord, if God be with us, why then is all of this befallen us? And where are all His wondrous works which our fathers told us of, saying: did not God bring us up from Egypt? But now God has cast us off, and delivered us into the hand of Midian." And God turned towards him and said: "Go in this your might, and save Israel from the hand of Midian. I herewith make you my messenger." And God said to him: "Surely I will be with you, and you shall smite the Midianites as one man." And he said to him: "If I have now found favor in your sight, then show me a sign that it is you that talks to me. Depart not hence, I pray you, until I come to you, and bring forth my present, and lay it before you." And he said: "I will tarry until you come back." And Gideon went in, and made ready a kid, and unleavened cakes of an ephah of meal. The flesh he put in a basket and he put the broth in a pot, and brought it to him under the terebinth, and presented it. And the angel of God said to him: "Take the flesh and the un-

leavened cakes, and lay them upon this rock, and pour
out the broth." And he did so. Then the angel of God
put forth the end of the staff that was in his hand, and
touched the flesh and the unleavened cakes. And fire
went up from out of the rock and consumed the flesh
and the unleavened cakes. And the angel of God departed out of his sight. And Gideon saw that he was
the angel of God and said: "Alas, O God. Forasmuch as
I have seen the angel of God face to face." And God
said to him: "Peace be unto you, and do not be afraid,
for you shall not die." Then Gideon built an altar to
God and called it "Adonai Shalom" . . . [Judg. 6:11–
24]

In an interesting story from an obscure Midrash,
Abrabanel presented the reason why Gideon was chosen
by the angel to be the deliverer of the Israelites from the
Midianites. The Midrash remarks that the angel waited
to hear the end of a conversation taking place between
Gideon and his father in a winepress, where the two of
them were threshing wheat. Gideon was saying, "Father,
you are too old for this work. Go home and rest and leave
the threshing to me. If the Midianites come, I will deal with
them." The angel was most impressed with Gideon's obvious love for his father and personal courage, and decided
right then that Gideon was the most qualified man to be
Israel's deliverer.

In this most unusual and graphic angelic encounter,
Gideon was not persuaded to carry out his mission until he
was fully assured that the voice that he heard was none
other than an angel of God. He asked to be given a sign as a
guarantee that this experience was a genuine one. It was
not at all unusual for biblical characters to be given a sign
as an assurance. Both Moses and the prophet Samuel received them. In our story Gideon brought a sacrificial offer-

ing of meat and bread, which when touched by the angel with his staff consumed the food in a fire. Thereupon the angel vanished and God spoke directly to Gideon, assuring him that he had nothing to fear and that he would not die. It was then that God began to directly communicate with Gideon.

Here again the angel of God simply acted as God's messenger. There are several details of the call to Gideon which are reminiscent of Moses' appointment to lead Israel out of Egypt. Both Moses and Gideon were provided with divine signs as well as the same phrase of assurance by God "and I will be with you."

Manoah's Angel

Manoah was the father of Samson, whose birth was foretold by an angel. Chapter 13 of the Book of Judges provides us with the details:

> And there was a certain man of Zorah, of the family of the Danites, whose name was Manoah. His wife was barren and she was unable to bear children. And the angel of God appeared to the woman, saying, "Behold, you are barren and have not borne. But you shall conceive and bear a son. Now, therefore, I pray you, do not drink strong wine or drink, nor eat any unclean thing. For you shall conceive and bear a son, and no razor shall come upon his head. For the child shall be a nazirite unto God from the womb, and he shall begin to save Israel from the hands of the Philistines." The woman came and told her husband, saying, "A man of God came to me, and his countenance was like the countenance of the angel of God, awesome. And I did not ask him from whence he came or what was his

name. But he said to me: 'Behold, you shall conceive and bear a son, and now drink no wine nor strong drink, and do not eat any unclean thing. For the child shall be a nazirite to God from the womb to the day of his death.'"

Then Manoah entreated God, and said: "O God, I pray You, let the man of God whom You did send come again to us, and teach us what we shall do to the child that shall be born." And God listened to the voice of Manoah, and the angel of God came again to the woman as she sat in the field. But Manoah her husband was not with her. And the woman made haste and ran and told her husband, saying, "Behold, the man has appeared to me that came to me that day." And Manoah arose and went after his wife, and came to the man, and said to him: "Are you the man that spoke to the woman?" And he said, "I am." And Manoah said, "Now, when your word comes to pass, what shall be the rule for the child, and what shall be done with him?" And the angel of God said to Manoah: "Of all that I have said to the woman, let her beware. She may not eat of anything that comes of the grapevine, neither let her drink wine nor strong drink, nor eat any unclean thing. All that I commanded her let her observe." And Manoah said to the angel of God: "I pray you, let us detain you, that we may make ready a kid for you." And the angel of God said to Manoah, "Though you detain me, I will not eat of your bread. And if you will make ready a burnt offering, you must offer it to God." For Manoah knew not that he was the angel of God. And Manoah said to the angel of God: "What is your name, that when your words come to pass we may honor you?" And the angel of God said: "Wherefore ask you after my name, seeing it is hidden?" So Manoah took the kid with the meal offering and offered it upon the rock to God. And the angel of God did wondrously, and Manoah and his wife looked on. For it came to pass that when the flame went up toward heaven from off the altar, that the angel of God ascended in the flame of the altar. And Manoah and his wife looked on, and they fell on their faces to the ground. But the angel of God did no more appear to Manoah or to his wife. Then Manoah knew that he was the angel of God. [Judg. 13:3–22]

Once again in this story, the angel of God acted as God's messenger, providing a sign to both Manoah and his wife by ascending in the flame of the altar. The angel had no identity, and once delivering the two-fold message that the woman would bear a son who should be raised as a nazirite (i.e. one who is consecrated to God) vanished never to be seen again. The Midrash (Numbers 10, 5) states that the appearance of the angel to Manoah's wife, a woman, is an indication of her high status in the community. When the angel of God directs Manoah's sacrifice to God Himself the indication is clearly that the angel is simply God's courier.

Isaiah's Angels

Isaiah, the first major prophet, lived in the eighth century B.C.E. He received the call to his prophetic mission in the closing year of the life of Uzziah or Azariah (740–739 B.C.E.). His divine calling, early in his manhood, is described in graphic detail in chapter 6 of his book when one day, while sitting in the Temple, he heard angels sing, "Holy, holy, holy is Adonai Tzeva'ot, the whole earth is full of God's glory." Here, now is the complete story:

In the year that King Uzziah died I saw God sitting
upon a throne high and lifted up, and God's train filled
the temple. Above Him stood the seraphim, each one
had six wings: with twain he covered his face, and
with twain he covered his feet, and with twain he did
fly. And one called unto the other saying: "Holy, holy,
holy is Adonai Tzeva'ot, the whole earth is full of
God's glory." And the posts of the door were moved at
the voice of them that called, and the house was filled
with smoke. Then I said: "Woe is me, for I am lost. I am
a man of unclean lips and I live among a people of
unclean lips. Yet my own eyes have beheld the King
Lord of Hosts." Then one of the seraphs flew over to
me with a live coal, which he had taken from the altar
with a pair of tongs. He touched it to my lips and
declared, "Now that this has touched your lips, your
guilt shall depart and your sin shall be purged." Then I
heard the voice of God saying, "Whom shall I send?
Who will go for us?" And I said, "Here am I, send me."
[Isa. 6:1–8]

In prophetic ecstasy, the heretofore unseen spiritual
world began to open up to Isaiah. Isaiah beheld God enthroned as the Sovereign on His throne and a class of
winged angels called "seraphim" calling to each other that
the whole world is filled with God's Divine Presence. Isaiah, overwhelmed by his unworthiness, admits to having
unclean lips. As a solution to Isaiah's problem, a seraph
with a glowing stone touches Isaiah's mouth, thus purging
him from any sin and impurity. Cleansed of human impurity, Isaiah is ready to answer God's call with the Hebrew
words reminiscent of Abraham's calling "hineni"—"here I
am, send me."
In this episode, unlike those previous stories where they

appeared in the guise of humans, the angels were depicted as composite semi-divine beings with three pairs of wings. These angels, called "seraphim," stand, fly, and proclaim God's ineffable holiness before the Divine throne. In addition to providing God with a chorus of voices, the angels, acting again as God's agents, are also able to prepare Isaiah for his mission by cleansing him of his perceived unholiness and unworthiness through a symbolic act of purification.

Ezekiel's Angels

Ezekiel, who was among the Judeans taken into Babylonian captivity in the year 597 B.C.E., was the first prophet to live and prophesy in exile. One of his most remarkable visions, indeed one of the most fantastic visions of any prophet to have ever lived, is described in the opening chapter of his book. It is the vision of the Divine Throne-Chariot, a mysterious apparition that gave rise to a system of mystical esoteric thought called "Ma'aseh Merkavah" ("dealings of the chariot"), which to this day is a part of the deliberations of Jewish mystics. Here is Ezekiel's vision at the commencement of his prophetic ministry:

> It came to pass in the thirtieth year . . . that the heavens were opened, and I saw visions of God . . . And I looked and behold a stormy wind came out of the north, a great cloud, with a fire flashing up, so that a brightness was around about it. . . . And out of the midst thereof came the likeness of four living creatures. And this was their appearance: they had the likeness of a man. And every one of them had four faces, and every one of them had four wings. And their feet were straight feet, and the sole of their feet was

like the sole of a calf's foot. And they sparkled like the
color of burnished brass. And they had the hands of a
man under their wings on their four sides. And as for
the faces and wings of them four. Their wings were
joined one to another. They did not turn when they
went. Each one went straight forward. As for the likeness of their faces, they had the face of a man. And the
four had the face of a lion on the right side, and the
four had the face of an ox on the left side. The four also
had the face of an eagle. Thus were their faces, and
their wings were stretched upward. Two wings of everyone were joined one to another and two covered
their bodies. Every one went straight forward . . . As
for the likeness of the living creatures, their appearance was like coals of fire, burning like the appearance
of torches. It flashed up and down among the living
creatures. And there was brightness to the fire, and out
of the fire went forth lightning. And the living creatures ran and returned as the appearance of a flash of
lightning. Now as I beheld the living creatures, behold
one wheel was at the bottom on the ground next to
the living creatures, at the four faces thereof. The appearance of the wheels and structure was like the
color of a beryl. The four had one likeness. Their appearance and their work was as it were a wheel within
a wheel . . . As for their rings, they were high and
dreadful. . . . Over the heads of the living creatures
was the likeness of a firmament, like the color of the
terrible ice, stretched forth above their heads. And
under the firmament were their wings conformable
the one to another . . . And when they went, I heard
the noise of their wings like the noise of great waters,
like the voice of the Almighty . . . When they stood,
they let down their wings . . . As the appearance of
the bow that is in the cloud in a rainy day, so was the

appearance of the brightness round about. This was the appearance of the likeness of the glory of God. And when I saw it, I fell upon my face, and I heard a voice of one that spoke. Then a spirit lifted me up and I heard behind me the voice of a great rushing: "Blessed be the glory of God from His place." [Ezek. 1:1, 4–11, 13–16, 19, 20, 22, 24, 28 and Ezek. 3:12]

No prophet was endowed with such an extreme vision as that of Ezekiel in the first chapter of his book. It reads like a feverish hallucination. Rabbinic tradition has relegated the study of God's Throne Chariot to people of the highest degree of mental and moral perfection. Clearly the fear was that if undertaken by less capable people, such investigation could lead to emotional imbalance and instability.

The main feature of the Divine Throne, drawn by the four-faced living creatures was its mobility, and this explains the wheels in Ezekiel's vision. No wheels were seen by Isaiah in his vision of the Divine Throne in chapter 6 or by any other prophet.

The bodies of the angelic beings stood upright and were shaped like the human body, but some of the faces resembled those of various animals. The creatures were not stationary, but galloped to and fro with the speed of lightning, making a great deal of noise with their flapping wings. The whole mechanism appeared to be rolling toward him rapidly, accompanied by thunder and lightning. Ezekiel took this figure on the throne to be God. He threw himself down on the ground to avoid being crushed by the storm cloud. At the conclusion of this particular vision, Ezekiel felt himself lifted up. The only words uttered by the angelic beings were the words of praise, "Blessed be the glory of God from His place."

Ezekiel may have been the first of the Jewish people to

have recorded an account of a direct visual and mystical encounter with God. As a result of the whole experience, he was transformed into a prophet, and proceeded throughout his book to warn the Israelite community of exiles of the impending destruction of Jerusalem.

Rabbinic commentators have stated that the four living creatures described in Ezekiel's vision were none other than cherubim. In addition, it has been conjectured that the main elements of the symbolism are suggested by the two colossal cherubim in the Temple in Jerusalem and partly by the composite winged figures which formed such an impressive feature in the palaces of Babylonia. It is also likely that the four hands on each side of the angelic beings and the wheels full of eyes were symbolic of the universality of the Divine presence.

Ezekiel's experience has served as a paradigm for other Jewish mystics to follow. The practice of attempting to ascend through the heavens and palaces was seen as an attempt to replicate that which had occurred to Ezekiel spontaneously. This became known as "heichalot" ("palace") or "chariot" mysticism.

This extraordinary experience and theophany of Ezekiel was chosen to be read each festival of Shavuot as the Haftarah, the prophetic portion, following the reading from the Torah scroll on that day of the Ten Commandments.

Zechariah's Angels

The Book of Zechariah is the eleventh of the "Twelve Prophets." The most characteristic feature of the prophecies of Zechariah is the visions. They were personal revelations, and the prophet was taught to see in these images a divine message which he in turn passed on to the Israelites. Of course the older prophets also saw visions, but in them angels hardly ever appeared. With Zechariah, angels were a constant feature and there is usually an interpreting angel present throughout each of the visions who took no role in the action, but rather served to explain what is going on. "The angel that spoke with me" is the language that was often used in these visions. The visions, of the nature of brief parables, ranged in theme from picturing the restoration of the exiles to announcing the overthrow of the heathen nations. Here are several examples:

The Four Horns and the Four Craftsmen:

I lifted up my eyes and saw and behold four horns. And I said to the angel that spoke with me: "What are these?" And he said to me: "These are the horns which have scattered Judah, Israel and Jerusalem." And God showed me four craftsmen. Then said I: "What come these to do?" and he spoke, saying: "These, the horns which scattered Judah, so that no person did lift up his head, these then are come to frighten them, to cast down the horns of the nations, which lifted up their horn against the land of Judah to scatter it." And I lifted up my eyes, and saw, and behold a man with a measuring line in his hand. Then said I: "Whither do you go?" And he said to me: "To measure Jerusalem, to see what is the breadth thereof, and what is the length thereof." And behold, the angel that spoke with me went forth, and another angel went out to meet him. [Zech. 2:1–7]

In this vision of the four horns and the four craftsmen, the theme is that the enemy forces (represented by the horns) that put Israel to flight will now themselves be overthrown by the angels (represented by the craftsmen) of God. The craftsmen represent the agencies by which the enemies of Israel will be overthrown. According to W. E. Barnes, a Christian Hebraist, the four craftsmen represent builders and artisans who will take a major role in the rebuilding of the Temple. They are four in number to signify that they come from the four corners of the earth. Interestingly, in the Talmud (*Sukkah 52b*), the four craftsmen are identified with the Messiah the son of David, the Messiah the son of Joseph, the prophet Elijah and the Righteous Priest (or Melchizedek), who represented the best type of monotheist among non-Israelite peoples.

The Golden Lamp:

Zechariah's vision of the golden lamp occurred in the early part of the fourth chapter of his book. In it the prophet saw a seven-branched golden candlestick which had an unfailing supply of oil:

> And the angel that spoke with me returned, and awakened me, as a man that is wakened out of his sleep. And he said to me, "What do you see?" And I said: "I have seen and behold a candlestick of gold, with a bowl on the top of it, and its seven lamps thereon. There are seven pipes, yea, seven to the lamps, which are upon the top thereof. And two olive trees by it, one on the right side of the bowl, and the other on the left side." And I answered and spoke to the angel that spoke with me, saying: "What are these, my lord?" Then the angel that spoke with me answered and said to me, "Do you not know what these are?" And I said, "No, my lord." Then he answered and spoke to me, saying: "This is the word of God to Zerubbabel, saying, 'Not by might, nor

by power, but by My spirit, says the Lord of Hosts.'"
[Zech. 4:1–7]

In this vision the prophet's thoughts turned to Zerubbabel (grandson of King Jehoichin and one of the first Jews
to return to Judea from Babylon) and the need to encourage him in his work. Zechariah saw a seven-branched
golden candelabrum which has an unending oil supply.
Above the candlestick was a bowl, and to the right and left
two olive trees that fed the bowl through two spouts. The
candlestick has been said to symbolize the restored Jewish
state which received God's grace through the prince and
the priest, both the civic and religious leaders of the community. The vision concluded with the famous message of
encouragement to Zerubbabel, "not by might nor by
power, but by My spirit, says the Lord of Hosts." This was
clearly a caution to Zerubbabel not to rely on force and
brute power but upon God's spirit when working to restore the kingdom. Rashi, the medieval commentator, explained that, just as the lamp in Zechariah's vision was fed
with oil not by man's hand and without human effort, so
too the Temple will be restored not by the strength of
Zerubbabel's hands but rather by the spirit of God. The
Haftarah selection chosen for the Sabbath of Hanukkah is
Zechariah's vision of the candlestick. Indeed the success of
the Maccabees was due in great part to their never-ending
faith and trust in God, thus creating an excellent theme
link between the story of Hanukkah, the rekindling of the
Temple *menorah* and the vision of Zechariah's candlestick.

Zechariah's Angel of the Lord and the Heavenly Horses:

For the first time in the Bible angels in Zechariah began to
appear to take on an independent life all of their own, with

the angel of the Lord appearing several times. In this first
example the angel acted both as the representative of God
and the advocate of Israel, interceding with God on behalf
of Israel. Rashi maintained that this particular angel of the
Lord was the interpreting angel who accompanied
Zechariah:

> I saw in the night, and behold a man riding upon a
> red horse, and he stood among the myrtle trees that
> were in the bottom. And behind him there were
> horses, red, sorrel and white. Then I said: "Oh my lord,
> what are these?" And the angel that spoke with me
> said to me: "I will show you what these are." And they
> answered the angel of the Lord that stood among the
> myrtle trees and said: "We have walked to and fro
> through the earth, and behold, all of the earth sits still
> and is at rest." Then the angel of the Lord spoke and
> said: "O God of Hosts, how long will You not have
> compassion on Jerusalem and on the cities of Judah,
> against which You have had anger these three score
> years and ten?" And God answered the angel that
> spoke with me with good words, even comforting
> ones. So the angel that spoke with me said to me:
> "Proclaim, saying: Thus says the Lord of Hosts: 'I am
> jealous for Jerusalem and for Zion with a great jeal-
> ousy. And I am very displeased with the nations that
> are at ease, first I was but a little displeased, and they
> helped for evil. Therefore, thus says God: I return to
> Jerusalem with compassion: My house shall be built in
> it, says the Lord of Hosts, and a line shall be stretched
> forth over Jerusalem.' Again, proclaim, saying: 'Thus
> says the Lord of Hosts: My cities shall again overflow
> with prosperity, and God shall yet comfort Zion, and
> shall yet choose Jerusalem.'" [Zech. 1:8–17]

Here we clearly see that the angel of the Lord acted as an interpreter for Zechariah. According to the seventeenth-century commentary of the *Metsudat David*, the interpreting angel of the Lord provided the answer to the prophet's question, "O lord, what are these?" by causing him to over-hear the conversation of the angelic riders. Not only did the angel of the Lord intercede on behalf of the Israelites, asking for God's compassion, but the angel of the Lord instructed Zechariah to tell the people that God's anger would soon be manifested toward all of the nations that so cruelly oppressed Israel. In the end, all of the Israelite cities would return to a state of prosperity.

The Angel of the Lord and the Charge Against Joshua:

In this vision of Zechariah, the High Priest Joshua was arraigned before the Heavenly Tribunal, with Satan the accuser (further details will be provided about Satan in the section of this volume on demonology):

And he showed me Joshua the High Priest standing before the angel of the Lord, and Satan standing at his right hand to accuse him. And God said to Satan: "God rebuke you, O Satan, the God that has chosen Jerusalem rebuke you. Is not this the man, a brand plucked out of fire?" Now Joshua was clothed with filthy garments, and stood before the angel. And he answered and spoke to those that stood before him, saying: "Take the filthy garments from off him." And he said to him: "Behold, I cause your iniquity to pass from you, and I will clothe you with robes." And I said: "Let them set a fair mitre upon his head, and clothe him with garments." And the angel of the Lord stood by.

And the angel of the Lord forewarned Joshua saying: "Thus says the Lord of Hosts: If you will walk in My ways, and if you will keep My charge, and will also judge My house, and will also keep My courts, then I will give you free access among these that stand by. Hear now, O Joshua the High Priest, you and your fellows that sit before you; for they are men that are a sign; for behold, I will bring forth My servant the Shoot." [Zech. 3:1–10]

According to David Kimchi, a twelfth century Spanish commentator, the angel of the Lord represented God and spoke in God's name as the judge. Joshua the High Priest was the accused, and Satan was the accuser, acting as a prosecuting attorney. Although the nature of the charge against Joshua is not specified, Jewish traditional commentators (including Rashi and Kimchi) have seen Joshua's guilt in the fact that his sons had married foreign women. Abraham Ibn Ezra, an eleventh century Spanish biblical commentator, refuted this position by stating that the sin of Joshua did not take place during his life. His view was that Satan represented the opposition of the enemies of Judah to the rebuilding of the Temple and their hostility to Joshua assuming the position of High Priest. Some commentators have maintained that the accusation was not directed against Joshua as an individual, but as the representative of the Israelite people who had been defiled in exile and upon whom the sins of their ancestors still rested. The vision proceeded by the angel of the Lord asking Joshua to remove his dirty clothing, symbolic of the sinfulness of the people. Joshua then requested that a pure diadem be placed on his head. As the angel of the Lord stood by, Joshua was clothed in priestly garments and the pure diadem on his head. Joshua then received the charge of the angel, assured that if he walked in God's ways, he would rule in God's house and have the privilege of direct communion with God. The vision concluded with a promise that the restored priesthood would be an omen for the advent of the Messiah.

Again in this vision, like the previous one, the angel of the Lord, presiding over the rehabilitation of Joshua the High Priest acquired some independence. Acting as God's attendant, messenger, and facilitator, the angel of the Lord spoke, rebuked the Satan for accusing Joshua, and fore-warned. For the first time in the Bible, the angels appeared to be much more autonomous, almost appearing to have acquired an independent life of their own.

Daniel's Angels

The Book of Daniel, belonging to the books of the Minor Prophets, consists of twelve chapters in two parts. It tells of a young Jew who, in the years following the Babylonian exile (586 B.C.E.), rose to a position of great power under the Persian king Darius. The first half of the book, written chiefly in Aramaic, the adopted speech of the Israelites after the Babylonian captivity, tells of the miraculous deliverance of Daniel and his three friends who were exiled to Babylon by King Nebuchadnezzar before the fall of Judea. It also includes Daniel's interpretation of Nebuchadnezzar's dreams. The last six chapters are apocalyptic writings, professing to reveal the future.

The Book of Daniel repeats much about angels which is found in earlier parts of the Bible. For example, it tells of innumerable attendants around the Divine throne: "A fiery stream issued, and came forth from before him. Thousand thousands ministered to him, and ten thousand times ten thousand stood before him" (Dan. 7:10).

The Vision of the Fiery Furnace:

In Daniel 3:25–28, an angel was reported to save three men (Shadrach, Meshach, and Abednego) in a fiery furnace:

> He [Nebuchadnezzar] answered and said: "Lo, I see four men loose, walking in the midst of the fire, and they have not been hurt, and the appearance of the fourth is like a son of the gods." Then Nebuchadnezzar came near to the mouth of the burning fiery furnace and he spoke and said: "Shadrach, Meshach and Abednego, you servants of God Most High, come forth and come here." Then Shadrach, Meshach and Abednego came forth out of the midst of the fire . . . And Nebuchadnezzar spoke and said: "Blessed be the God of Shadrach, Meshach and Abednego, who has sent His angel, and delivered His servants that trusted in Him, and have changed the king's word, and have yielded their bodies, that they might not serve nor worship any god, except their own God." [Dan. 3:26–3:28]

In this vision, King Nebuchadnezzar, who had hoped that his threat to burn the three Jews alive would be effective when they obstinately refused to worship his idol, became witness to the miraculous deliverance of the Jews from the fiery furnace. He reacted to the miracle by praising the God of the three Jewish men who had sent His angel to save them.

Daniel in the Lion's Den:

In chapter 6 of the book, Daniel found himself sentenced to death, having been thrown into a den of lions:

And when he came near to the den to Daniel, he cried with a pained voice. The king spoke and said to Daniel: "O Daniel, servant of the living God, is your God who you serve continually able to deliver you from the lions?" Then Daniel said to the king: "O king, live forever! My God has sent His angel, and has shut the lions' mouths, and they have not hurt me." [Dan. 6:20–6:22]

As in the vision of the fiery furnace, God's angel again came to perform his miraculous saving work. This resulted in King Darius' decision to cast all of Daniel's accusers into the lion's den. In addition, Darius, now totally convinced of God's great power, made a decree ordering all the people in the kingdom to proclaim God as an eternal deliverer whose dominion would reign forever. The angel, acting strictly as an agent of God, neither spoke nor demonstrated any autonomy. In the end, however, it was the angel, and not God, who effected the rescue of Daniel.

The Book of Daniel presents many new features with regard to angels. The revelations received by Daniel were either symbolic visions in which an angel interpreted (vision of the ram and he-goat in chapter 8), or they were revealed in their entirety by an angel, such as those visions in chapters 10–12. Zechariah, too, had visions which an angel explained. However, he also delivered prophecies received directly from God, which did not occur in the Book of Daniel. Also in the Book of Daniel 4:13, angels of God did not merely carry out orders, but had some autonomy and powers of initiative: "The matter has been decreed by the watchers, and the sentence by the word of the holy ones."

There are two most unique features of the book of Daniel vis-à-vis angels which make it truly noteworthy. First, it is the only book of the Bible in which angels have distinct personalities and are even given the proper names of Michael and Gabriel. In addition, the idea that each nation has an angelic sponsor and patron whose actions and destinies are bound up with those of his nation is encountered for the first time in the book.

Michael and Gabriel

The angels Michael and Gabriel act as vision interpreters in addition to announcing futuristic events. It is in chapter 8 of the Book of Daniel that an angel, (Gabriel) is named in the Bible.

Vision of the Rams and He-Goat:

And it came to pass, when I, Daniel had seen the vision, that I sought to understand it. And behold, there stood before me as the appearance of a man. And I heard the voice of a man between the banks of Ulai, who called and said: "Gabriel, make this man to understand the vision." So he came near where I stood and when he came, I was terrified, and fell upon my face. But he said to me: "Understand, O son of man. For the vision belongs to the time of the end." Now as he was speaking with me, I fell into a deep sleep with my face toward the ground. But he touched me, and set me upright. And he said: "Behold, I will make you know what shall be in the latter time of the indignation. For it belongs to the appointed time of the end. The ram which you saw having two horns, they are the kings of Media and Persia. And the rough he-goat, is the king of Greece. And the great horn that is between his eyes is the first king. And as for that which was broken, in the place whereof four stood up, four kingdoms shall stand up out of the nation, but not with his power. And in the latter time of their kingdom, when the transgressors have completed their transgression, there shall stand up a king of fierce countenance, and understanding stratagems." [Dan. 8:15–23]

Vision of the Seventy Heptads:

While Daniel was trying to fathom the meaning of the vision of the ram and the he-goat, an anonymous angel appeared before him, telling him that his vision foretold the future (i.e. that the history of the pagan kingdoms would come to an end when God intervened to destroy the persecutor). The anonymous angel called to another angel, named Gabriel, who was asked to explain the vision to Daniel.

Gabriel again appeared in human form in the Book of Daniel (9:21). There his task was to explain the seventy-week period decreed upon the Jewish people to allow them time to end their transgressions:

While I was speaking in prayer, the man Gabriel, whom I had seen in the vision at the beginning, being caused to fly swiftly, approached close to me about the time of the evening offering. And he made me to understand, and talked with me, and said: "O Daniel, I am now come forth to make you skilled in understanding . . . Seventy weeks are decreed upon your people and upon your holy city, to finish the transgression and to make an end of sin, and to forgive iniquity, and to bring in everlasting righteousness, and to seal vision and prophet, and to anoint the most holy place. Know therefore and discern, that from the going forth of the word to restore and to build Jerusalem unto one anointed, a prince shall be seven weeks, and for three-score and two weeks, it shall be built again, with broad place and moat, but in troubled times. And after the threescore and two weeks shall an anointed one be cut off, and be no more. And the people of a prince that shall come shall destroy the city and the sanctu-ary. But his end shall be with a flood, and unto the end of the war desolations are determined. And he shall make a firm covenant with many for one week. And for half of the week he shall cause the sacrifice and the offering to cease . . ." [Dan. 9:20–27]

At the beginning of Daniel's prayer, the answer to his prayer was given by God in the form of an oracle, heard by the angels assisting at the Divine throne. The angel Gabriel (literally meaning "man of God") was commissioned by God to convey this oracle to Daniel. Daniel was told that the expression "seventy years" really meant only seventy weeks. The angel Gabriel was also able to fly, and more than a simple interpreter depicted the future event of a rebuilt Jerusalem, a thought likely to comfort the hearts of the Israelites during the dark period of the Maccabees.

First Vision of Michael:

The prince of the kingdom of Persia withstood me one and twenty days; but lo, Michael, one of the chief princes, came to help me. And I was left over there beside the kings of Persia. Now I am come to make you understand what shall befall your people in the ends of days. For there is yet a vision for the days. And when he had spoken to me according to these words, I set my face toward the ground, and was dumb. And behold, one like the similitude of the sons of men touched my lips. Then I opened my mouth, and spoke and said to him that stood before me: "O my lord, by reason of the vision my pains are come upon me, and I retain no strength. For how can this servant of my lord talk with this my lord? For as for me, straightaway there remained no strength in me, neither was there breath left in me." Then there touched me again one like the appearance of a man, and he strengthened me. And he said, "O man greatly beloved, do not be afraid. Peace be unto you, be strong, yea be strong." And when he had spoken to me, I was strengthened and said, "Let my lord speak, for you have strengthened me." Then he said: "Do you know why I have come to you? Now I will return to fight with the prince of Persia. And when I go forth, lo, the prince of Greece shall come. Howbeit I will declare to you that which is inscribed in the writing of truth. And there is none that holds with me against these, except Michael your prince.

And as for me, in the first year of Darius the Mede, I stood up to be a supporter and a stronghold to him. Now I will declare to you the truth. Behold, there shall stand up yet three kings in Persia. And the fourth shall be far richer than all of them. And when he is waxed strong through his riches, he shall stir up all against the realm of Greece. And a mighty king shall stand up, that shall rule with great dominion, and do according to his will. And when he shall stand up, his kingdom shall be broken, and shall be divided toward the four winds of heaven. But not to his posterity, nor according to his dominion wherewith he ruled, for his kingdom shall be plucked up, even for others beside these." [Dan. 10:13–11:4]

The "prince of the kingdom of Persia" mentioned in the opening of this vision is not considered to be King Cyrus of

Persia, but rather the tutelary spirit or guardian angel of the Persian kingdom according to rabbinic commentary. In like manner, rabbinic commentary has considered Michael as the guardian angel of the Jewish people and so is called "one of the chief princes." Belief in guardian angels for all nations survives from ancient polytheistic theology which held that each city-state or nation had a tutelary god who was in a particular way its protector, enjoying special status. Guardian angels in Israelite tradition were always made subject to God's supreme authority. Although they had some modicum of self-authority and independence, they were, in the long run, always acting as agents of God, Who had ultimate control over them.

In this vision of Daniel, the guardian angel identified as Michael (meaning "who is like God") had come to explain what the future had in store for Israel. Upon seeing a celestial being in the form of a man of dazzling appearance, Daniel became terrified. At the sound of the angel's voice Daniel fell prostrate to the ground. The angel touched him and reassured him that all was well. The angel then told him about the war in heaven between the prince of the kingdom of Persia and himself. There followed a select survey of history as it affects the fortune of the Jewish people. Four Persian kings would arise, and the fourth (identified by some as Xerxes or Ahasuerus in the Book of Esther) would acquire the greatest riches of them all. Another king (often identified as Alexander the Great) would then arise, but his vast domain would be divided up. The vision continued with more details related to the future course of events affecting the Jewish people.

Vision of the Resurrection of the Dead:

In the last chapter of the Book of Daniel, the final words of the angel Michael's revelation are presented:

At that time shall Michael stand up, the great prince who stands for the children of your people. And there shall be a time of trouble, such as never was since there was a nation even to that same time. And at that time your people shall be delivered, every one that shall be found written in the book. And many of them that sleep in the dust of the earth shall awaken, some to everlasting life, and some to reproaches and abhorrence. And they that are wise shall shine as the brightness of the firmament, and they that turn the many to righteousness as the stars for ever and ever. But you, O Daniel, shall shut up the words, and seal the book, even to the time of the end. Many shall run to and fro, and knowledge shall be increased. [Dan. 12:1–4]

The time frame of this last vision is generally undertood to be the period after the death of Antiochus. Those Jews who suffered such cruel persecution under this cruel king's reign would now be rewarded for their fidelity not here on earth but beyond the grave. The wise leaders would be distinguished from the rest of the faithful because they would shine brightly, and those who led the multitude to righteousness would be like the stars. It certainly must have been a comforting thought for the people to know that ultimately righteous people will in the end triumph, and that there would be a resurrection of the dead, because so many suffered martyrdom in proof of their love for God. Some commentators have instructed that the stars symbolize the angels themselves. If this is true, then this group of righteous people shared in the same splendor of the angel. Now that the angel Gabriel had finished his revelation of the future course of history and had given assurance to Daniel of the ultimate victory of the righteous, he ordered Daniel to keep the words secret and seal the book until the final phase.

Michael and Gabriel appear again and again in the role of
guardian angels in post-biblical literature, including in the
Apocrypha, Talmud, Midrash, and among other Jewish
sects. They will be further discussed with more detail in
the forthcoming chapters of the book.

2

ANGELS AMONG
THE JEWISH SECTS

Belief and a view of angels was not common to the Jewish people as a whole. Indeed, the teachers of apocalyptic wisdom desired to impart their knowledge of angels to a narrow group of those who were specially initiated in the subject matter. Both the Sadducees and the Pharisees showed little interest in angel lore. Angelology did find its widest distribution among the secret societies of the Essenes, a religious sect at the close of the period of the Second Temple. They lived an abstemious communal life, carefully guarding the secret list of angels' names.

In 1947, ancient manuscripts were accidentally discovered in a cave at Qumran near the Dead Sea by an Arab shepherd boy. Other scrolls were later found, yielding a plethora of information that testified to an organized system of angelology. It has been considered scholarly opinion that the so-called "scroll people" belonged to the Jewish sect known as the Essenes.

The Essenes, in one of their scrolls entitled "The War of the Sons of Light Against the Sons of Darkness," wrote of the plan of the struggle of "the sons of the light" (i.e.

members of the sect) against "the sons of darkness" (i.e. those which had strayed from God's covenant led by the forces of Belial, the angel of darkness and his evil forces), which was to begin with the conquest of Palestine and to end forty years later with the conquest of the whole world. As a result of their dualistic outlook, the Essenes saw themselves as the chosen "sons of light" elected as such by God. It has been conjectured by some Dead Sea Scroll scholars that the concept of the sons of light and darkness in combat is in some way related to the Persian Zoroastrian doctrine of dualism which pits the god of light (Ahura Mazda) against the god of darkness (Ahriman).

The theme of angels of light and darkness fighting with each other is likewise expressed in a scroll entitled "The Manual of Discipline:" "In the hand of the Prince of Light is the dominion of all of the sons of righteousness . . . and in the hand of the angel of darkness is the dominion of the sons of evil." Some have supposed that the Prince of Light was Uriel, but others have said that he was Michael, for he is described in the War Scroll as being sent by God in "eternal light."

In sum, the Scroll people were quite certain that one day they would ultimately prevail over the forces of evil. The angelic armies of the Sons of Light would triumph, they believed, over the angels of destruction of the Sons of Darkness. This would lead to an era of personal salvation when all people would be blessed by a gathering of angels.

3

ANGELS IN THE APOCRYPHA
AND PSEUDEPIGRAPHA

The books of the Apocrypha, representing substantial ethical literature, reflect the developments of social and religious life among the Jewish people during the period of the Second Temple. Since these books were not included in the Hebrew Bible, the Talmud refers to them as "Sefarim Chitzonim" (outside books). They are also called books of the Apocrypha ("hidden away" in Greek), because they were produced after the time of Ezra the Scribe when direct revelation had ceased with the passing of the prophets. The Apocrypha's most famous books are the Books of the Maccabees, which tell the story of the Jewish revolt against King Antiochus, the Syrian king who tried to wipe out Judaism. The Hanukkah story and its hero Judah Maccabee are known to us largely through these books. The Apocrypha's next most famous book is Ecclesiasticus, also known as the Wisdom of Ben Sira. This book contains hundreds of proverbs and poems. Other books in the Apocrypha include two Books of Esdras, Tobit, and Judith. Most of the books of the Apocrypha were written by Jews in either Hebrew or Aramaic.

The Pseudepigrapha also consists of noncanonical Jewish literature written during the period of the Second Temple and some time after its destruction. The name denotes books ascribed to imaginary authors who take names from the great heroes of Israel's history. Among others, these include Moses, Abraham, Enoch, Solomon, Isaiah, and Ezra.

In most of these post-biblical books, angels appear with extreme frequency, often distinguishable by their own name and individual traits. This is due in part to the fact that during the period of the Second Temple, when these books were being composed, it was assumed that only the great prophets of earlier days had the privilege and ability to directly communicate with God. This created the necessity to use angels as intermediaries in order to teach the apocalyptic-type literature that dealt with the nature of heaven and the end of days. Angels were not only used, but their nature and individual characteristics were explored.

These post-biblical books were excluded from the Hebrew Bible because the rabbis considered them dangerous to Jewish faith. The concern was both the possibility of angel worship and their over-emphasis in apocalyptic matters.

Enoch's Angels

By means of the wisdom of the Chaldeans the Jews familiarized themselves well with a plethora of Babylonian myths, including the stories of creation and the flood, and sought to harmonize these myths with the biblical reports of these events. However, in order to avoid inconsistency with the monotheistic character of Judaism, the Jewish legends were ascribed to the world of angels. One such example was Enoch, a figure whose concept was created through Babylonian influence. Enoch was a figure who appeared as the creator of human culture and transmitter of heavenly wisdom to early man. His authority was completely derived by his ability to constantly communicate with angels. Two Jewish apocalyptic books are ascribed to him, filled with angel references.

The following is a listing of some of the angels that appear in the books of Enoch. Notice how the names of each of the angels bears the suffix "el," meaning God. In addition, each of their names indicates the mission to which each has been assigned:

Gabriel: Fire angel
Ruchiel: Angel of the wind
Ra'amiel: Angel of thunder
Shalgiel: Angel of snow
Matariel: Angel of precipitation
Lailiel: Night angel
Galgalliel: Angel overseeing sun's orb
Opaniel: Angel overseeing disk of moon
Barakiel: Lightning angel

In the biblical Book of Genesis 6:24, we are told that "Enoch walked with God, then he was no more, for God took him." This most unusual mysterious ending to his life led to the Pseudepigrapha version of the transporting of Enoch while alive to the sphere of the heavens. There, in Enoch 1, he reported the following: "I saw a hundred thousand times a hundred thousand, ten million times ten million, an innumerable multitude who stand before the presence of the God of the Spirits."

As the passage in Enoch 1 continues, Enoch identified four angels by name:

I saw them standing on the four wings of the God of the Spirits, and I saw four other faces among those who do not sleep, and I came to learn their names, which the angel who came to me revealed . . . I heard the voices of the four faces while they were singing praises before God of Glory . . . Afterwards, I asked the angel of peace who was going with me and showed me everything that was hidden: "Who are the four faces that I have seen?" And he said to me, "The first one is the merciful and forbearing Michael. The second one who is set over all disease and every wound of the children of the people is Raphael. The third, who is set over all exercise of strength is Gabriel. And the fourth, who is set over all actions of repentance to the hope of those who would inherit eternal life, is Phanuel (in other versions Uriel) by name."

The first book of Enoch also adds three additional angels to the four: Sariel, whose duties are not defined, Jeremiel, who is in charge of the souls of the netherworld, and Raguel, who takes revenge upon the world of lights.

Much like high level cabinet ministers of the president of the United States, these four archangels, closest to God's throne, serve as the inner advisory circle of God's presence. We shall now more carefully examine this exclusive quartet of angels.

The Four Archangels

Michael and Gabriel:

Michael and Gabriel, often paired together, were two of the four angels who surrounded the throne of the Almighty. First appearing in the book of Daniel, Michael was portrayed as the constant defender of the Jewish people in the *Peskita Rabbati,* an early medieval legendary work. Michael and Gabriel also appeared in a variety of other midrashic selections. For instance, in *Genesis Rabbah 48:9,* the midrashic commentary to the book of Genesis identifies Michael and Gabriel as two of three angels who visited Abraham after his circumcision. There Michael's task was to announce the future birth of Isaac while Gabriel's was to destroy Sodom. In the story of the wrestling of an angel with Jacob, *Genesis Rabbah 78:1* identified the unnamed adversary as either Michael or Gabriel. *Genesis Rabbah 59:10* also identifies Michael as the angel who accompanied Abraham's servant Eliezer on his mission to find a suitable wife for Isaac.

In *Esther Rabbah 10:9,* it was Michael who pushed Haman against Esther to make it appear as if Haman intended to violate her.

Michael and Gabriel also play an important role in the books of the Pseudepigrapha. In *3 Baruch,* he was the custodian of the keys to the heavenly kingdom. There, as well as in other places in the Pseudepigrapha, he was the angel who accepted the prayers of humans and communicated them to God. In the Book of Enoch, it was Gabriel who provided Enoch with courage as he got closer to the throne of God.

The motifs of Michael and Gabriel are also repeated in the Kabbalah's mystical tradition, but Michael is given added importance. Playing a central role in the realm of God's Divine Chariot, Michael is the guardian of the south side, the figure of the lion in the Chariot. Michael is also allotted the role of grace in the *Merkavah,* angel of the right, representing the Divine sphere of "chesed" (i.e. grace). Frequently described as a high priest, Michael is also portrayed in the *Book of the Zohar, (i.e. "book of mysticism"*) as bringing the souls of the righteous before God, an act which led to their inclusion in the kabbalistic world of emanation.

Raphael:

From the Hebrew word *refuah* (i.e. healing), Raphael was the angel of healing. The Talmud (*Yoma 37a*) knows him as one of the three angels who came to visit Abraham after he had circumcised himself at age ninety-nine. As a planetary angel he governs the sun, and in the division of the four corners of the world he commands the west. He is also one of the four angels of the Presence who stand on the four sides of God. In kabbalistic mystical literature, Raphael has a high rank and is credited with a variety of missions. Among the four elements, he governs earth. In the colors of the rainbow, he represents green. According to other mystics, he commands the special host of angels known as the *"Ophanim,"* which appeared in the opening chapter of Ezekiel's famous vision of God's Throne Chariot. In the Zohar itself, Raphael is the angel who dominates the morning hours, bringing relief to the ill.

Raphael also appears in the books of the Pseudepigrapha. He especially receives a fair amount of press in the apocryphal Book of Tobit. Tobit was a pious and charitable Jew who had been exiled by the Assyrian King Shalmanasser. His greatest capital offense was to bury his fellow Jews who had died. Having to escape with his wife, he eventually went blind and prayed to God that his life would be ended. His great love for his wife Hannah and his child Tobias was his only saving grace.

At the same time that Tobit said his prayer to God, Sarah, daughter of Tobit's brother, also prayed to God. She had the unfortunate task of having to bury seven of her husbands because they were all killed on her wedding nights by the evil demon Asmodeus. Here is her prayer:

> "You know God, Sarah prayed, that I am innocent of any sin with man. I have never defiled my name, or the name of my father, in the land of my captivity. I am my father's only child. I have already lost seven husbands. Why must I live any more?"

The prayers of both of them were heard in the presence of the glory of the great Raphael, and he was sent to cure them. For Tobit, to remove the white films over his eyes, and to give Sarah, the daughter of Raguel, to Tobit's son Tobias, as his wife, and to bind Asmodeus the wicked demon, because Tobias was entitled to possess her.

As the story played itself out, the angel Raphael, dressed in human disguise became Tobias's traveling partner. Raphael, using his powers of healing, performed his duty, exorcising Asmodeus from the soul of Sarah and restoring Tobit to full vision (Book of Tobit 3:14–15). In the end, Raphael revealed his true identity with these words: "I am Raphael, one of the seven holy angels, who offer up the prayers of God's people and go into the presence of the glory of the Holy One" (Book of Tobit 12:15).

Uriel:

Meaning "God is my light," Uriel appears in the *Midrash Rabbah* (*Num. 2:10*) as one of the four angels that God placed around His throne. *The Zohar,* the book of Jewish mysticism, not only identifies Uriel as one of the four beasts (sometimes the lion, and at other times the eagle) that Ezekiel saw in the first chapter of his book, but as one of the four angels that shed light on the four winds of heaven.

Uriel's light is considered the most perfect, and it is shed over the west. *The Zohar* (*1, 6b*) also ascribes to Uriel a special function in connection with the sacrifices during First Temple times. The altar, called "Ariel" in Isaiah 29, was named after Uriel, who descended in the guise of a lion to crouch on the altar and swallow sacrifices. Uriel's appearance in the altar fire caused all those who saw the flames to change their ways and repent.

Uriel also appears in several of the pseudepigraphic books. In the first Book of Enoch, Uriel served as his guide, along with the three other archangels, in the upper heavens. His particular function in that book was to govern the army of angels and the netherworld: "Uriel, whom the God of glory has set for ever over all of the luminaries of the heaven, in the heaven and in the world, that they should rule on the face of the heaven and be seen in the earth, and be leaders for the day and the night" (I Enoch 7:53).

A very specialized function was assigned to Uriel in the fourth book of Ezra (II Esdras). In this book, Uriel responded to Ezra's questions vis-à-vis the state of the world and God's plan for the people of Israel. By means of various visions he revealed to Ezra the duration of the present age and the place and role of the people of Israel in the future world.

Metatron

One angel accorded a distinctive role in Jewish angelology is the angel called Metatron, who plays a significant role in the Talmud, Pseudepigrapha, and Jewish mysticism. The origin of the name of this angel is obscure. Suggestions for its origin include the following: from the word "matar," meaning "keeper of the watch;" from the word "metator," meaning "a messenger or guide;" from the combination of the Greek words "meta" and "thronos," meaning "one who serves behind the throne."

In the Talmud, Metatron is mentioned in three places. In the tractate called *Hagigah 15a*, Elisha ben Avuyah saw Metatron seated and said that "perhaps there are two powers," as though indicating that Metatron himself is a second deity. The Talmud explains that Metatron was given permission to be seated because of his position as celestial scribe recording the good deeds of Israel. It was proven to Elisha that Metatron could not be a second deity based on the fact that Metatron received sixty blows with fiery rods to demonstrate that he was not a god, but an angel.

In the second story from the Talmudic tractate of *Sanhedrin 38b*, Metatron is described as the angel of God referred to in Exodus 23:21 of whom it was said, "do not listen to his voice."

Another tradition associates Metatron with Enoch who "walked with God" (Gen. 5:22) and who ascended to heaven, thus changing from a human to a celestial being. His roles were diverse, and included ministering to the Throne of Glory, acting as Temple high priest, acting as a minister of wisdom, and keeping charge of the guardian angels.

Some kabbalists often identified Metatron with the Supreme emanation of light from the Shechinah. Others identified Metatron the angel with Enoch, the one who ascended to heaven. *The Zohar* describes this transformation, stating that the Divine spark which God placed into Adam, the first human being, left his body after having sinned by eating of the Tree of Knowledge. The spark entered the body of Enoch, perfecting him to the point that he needed to be transported to heaven, and there he metamorphised into the angel Metatron.

In later literature the material relating to Metatron is scattered. However, there has been wide agreement among students of angels that there is hardly a duty in the celestial realm and within the dominion of one angel among the other angels in which Metatron is not involved.

4

THE RABBIS AND THE ANGELS

In the rabbinic age, belief in angels was general, among both scholars and the laity. There were, however, many differences of opinion among rabbinic thinkers as to the nature of angels. Some held the opinion that a new core of angels was created each and every day, whose task was to praise God and then to sink into a river of fire:

> Samuel said to Chiyya bar Rav: "O son of a lion of a man, come, and I will tell you some of the beautiful things your father used to say: 'Each and every day ministering angels are created from the fire river, utter songs, and then cease to be, as it is said, "Because they are new every morning, the praise of Your faithfulness is great"'" [Lamentations 3:23] (Talmud *Chagigah, 14a*). Others accepted this opinion, adding that only two angels, Michael and Gabriel, permanently served God, while all of the other angels sing their hymns of praise on the day of their creation and disappear.

Rabbinic Origin of Angels

Both the Talmud and the Midrash contain a variety of opinions on the origins and the nature of angels. Rabbi Yochanan stated that the angels were created on the second day of creation, whereas Rabbi Chanina stated that they were created on the fifth day (*Genesis Rabbah 1:3*).

The Talmudic tractate of *Chagigah 16a* discusses the continuous creation of angels, based on the fact that every pronouncement by God resulted in the creation of angels. We are told that angels walk upright, speak Hebrew, are endowed with understanding, can fly in the air, and can move from one end of the world to another, foretelling the future.

In the Jerusalem Talmud (*Rosh Hashanah 2*) we are told that angels have something in common with both men and demons. They have the shape of man but consist half of fire and half of water.

The *Midrash* (*Genesis Rabbah 48:11*) states that they enjoy the splendor of the Shechinah and are free of all evil inclination.

Here is a brief summary of the variety of rabbinic opinions related to angels as culled from Jewish rabbinic sources:

i. No angel may carry out more than one mission at a time (Talmud *Baba Metzia 86b*).

ii. Angels are capable of errors (*Ecclesiastes Rabbah 6:10*).

iii. The size of an angel is equal to a third of the world (*Genesis Rabbah 68:12*).

iv. The impulse to evil has no power over angels (*Genesis Rabbah 48:11*).

v. Angels have no backs and experience no weariness (Talmud *Chagigah 15a*).

vi. Angels are kept alive only by the splendor of the Presence of God (*Exodus Rabbah 32:4*).

vii. Every day, in the morning, an angel opens its mouth and says, "God reigns, God did reign, and God will reign forever and forever" (*Heichalot*).

viii. Angels must not take a step without God's command (*Tanchuma, B. Exodus 115*).

Rabbinic Classification of Angels

Just as there is a diversity of opinion regarding the origin of angels, so too there are a multitude of rabbinic classifications of angels. Rabbi Yochanan (*Tanchuma, B. Lev. 39*) was of the opinion that angels are divided into angels of peace and evil angels. The angels of peace dwell near God while the latter are remote from God. Rabbi Samuel ben Isaac (*Genesis Rabbah 9:10*) stated that there are also angels of life and angels of death.

Like the apocryphal literature, rabbinic midrashic works regard Gabriel, Michael, Raphael, and Uriel as the archangels, referring to them as the ministering angels:

Four companies of ministering angels utter praise before the Holy One, blessed be He: the first camp, that of Michael, at God's right; the second camp, that of Gabriel, at God's left; the third camp, that of Uriel, in front of God; and the fourth camp, that of Raphael, behind God. [*Pirke of Rabbi Eliezer, 4*]

In another Talmudic legend angels accompany people home on the eve of the Sabbath. Some have said that the

traditional hymn "Shalom Aleichem," which welcomes
ministering angels, was inspired from the following Talmudic legend about angels:

> It was taught, Rabbi Jose the son of Rabbi Judah
> said: Two ministering angels accompany a person on
> the eve of the Sabbath from the synagogue to the
> home, one a good [angel] and one an evil [one]. And
> when the person arrives home and finds the lamp
> burning, the table laid and the couch covered with
> a spread, the good angel exclaims, "May it be even
> thus on another Sabbath too," and the evil angel
> unwillingly responds "amen." But if not, the evil
> angel exclaims, "May it be even thus on another Sab-
> bath too," and the good angel unwillingly responds
> "amen." [Talmud *Shabbat 119b*]

This certainly provides incentive for persons to do the
"right thing" when it comes to proper observance of Sabbath ritual!

There are even occasions when God consults with the
angels, as God did before the creation of human beings:

> Rabbi Samuel ben Nachman said in Rabbi Yoch-
> anan's name: "When Moses was occupied in writing
> the Torah, he had to write the work of each day. When
> he came to the verse, And God said, Let us make man
> in our image, he said: 'Sovereign of the Universe! Why
> do You furnish an excuse to heretics? Write,' replied
> God; 'whoever wishes to make a mistake may do so.'
> 'Moses,' said God to him, 'this man that I have created,
> do I not cause men both great and small to spring from
> him? Now if a great man comes to obtain permission
> from one that is less than he, he may say, "Why should
> I ask permission from my inferior?" Then they will

answer him, "Learn from your Creator, who created all that is above and below, yet when God came to create human beings God took counsel with the ministering angels". [*Genesis Rabbah 8:5*]

In this Midrash it seems clear that the instruction to the reader is the value of modesty and humility. That is to say, even an all powerful God on occasion needs to consult others for advice!

There are also angels that control such matters as prayers, anger, birth and pregnancy, famine, rain, and hail. The following is a dialogue between the angel of hail and the angel Gabriel, each vying for the privilege of saving three righteous men from a fiery inferno:

When the wicked Nebuchadnezzar cast Hananiah, Mishael and Azariah into the fiery furnace, Yurkami, the angel prince of hail, appeared before the Holy One and said, "Master of the universe, let me go down, cool the furnace, and thus save those righteous men from the fiery furnace." Gabriel spoke up and said, "The might of the Holy One will not be made evident this way, for you are the prince of hail, and everyone knows that water quenches fire. But I am the prince of fire. Let me go down and I shall cook it within and heat it without, and thus perform a miracle within a miracle. . . ." [Talmud *Pesachim 118b*]

In the following talmudic story, angels worked to alleviate famine:

Rabbi Mari, the son of Samuel's daughter, related: "On that day I was standing on the bank of the river Papa and saw angels disguised as mariners bringing sand and loading ships with it, and the sand turned into fine flour. When everybody came to purchase it, I called out to them, 'Do not buy this flour, because it was produced by a miracle.' The next day, boatloads of rice came in." [Talmud *Taanit 24b*]

Guardian Angels

The concept of a guardian angel also permeates the Talmud and midrashic texts. For instance, in *Deuteronomy Rabbah 1:22,* we are informed that when Israel's enemy nations fall that the guardian angels will fall with them, and when they are punished, the angels also suffer punishment. In the talmudic tractate of *Yoma 77a,* we are surprised to learn that Dubiel, the guardian angel of the Persians, was known by name to the rabbis! The guardian angel of Edom is also mentioned in the Talmud *Makkot 12a.*

Sometimes the guardian angel of a people pleads on its behalf in order to avert divine punishment. At the time of the exodus from Egypt, the guardian angels of all of the nations were summoned by God to discuss God's quarrel with Egypt. During these discussions, the angel Gabriel, acting upon orders from Michael, produced a part of the wall which the Israelites had been forced to erect for the Egyptians. When it was discovered to contain the body of an Israelite child, punishment was meted out both to the guardian angel of Egypt and to the Egyptians themselves (*Yalkut Exodus 243*).

Kings were also said to have guardian angels. For example, King Nebuchadnezzar of Babylon had a guardian angel named Kal (*Exodus Rabbah 21: 5*). The seas had their own guardian angels (*Exodus Rabbah 15:22*). Frequent mention was also made of the angel or "Prince" of the world, known in Hebrew as "Sar" (*Exodus Rabbah 17:4*).

The Angel of Death ("malach hamavet" in Hebrew) plays a special role among the guardian angels and is regarded as the most heinous among all of the wicked angels. In the Talmud *Ketubot 77b,* Rabbi Joshua ben Levi encountered the Angel of Death while immersed in study. In the remarkable story that follows, Rabbi Joshua ben Levi was flown to the World to Come after having persuaded the death angel to give him his sword as surety that he would not die until his mission was completed. With sword in hand, Rabbi Joshua ben Levi entered Paradise, while the other celestial beings protested the entrance of a living person. God ordered Rabbi Joshua to return the sword to its rightful owner, thus concluding the story whose moral is that all humans are destined to die. More details concerning the role of the angel of death will be forthcoming in the section on Satan.

Angels and Their Work in Biblical and Post-Biblical Periods

There are numerous examples of legends which feature a variety of actions carried out by angels during the biblical and post-biblical periods. In *Genesis Rabbah 8:15,* the archangels Michael and Gabriel acted as sponsors at the wedding of Adam and Eve: "Rabbi Abbahu said: 'The Holy One, blessed be He, took a cup of blessing and blessed them.' R. Judah ben R. Simon said: 'Michael and Gabriel were Adam's best men.'"

In the Midrash of *Targum Jonathan, Genesis 4:1,* the angel Samael made Eve pregnant. In *Genesis Rabbah 25:1,* Enoch was taken from earth and ascended to heaven. There he was given the name of the angel Metatron.

In *Genesis Rabbah 78:2,* the angel who wrestled with Jacob sought to return to the celestial sphere in time to

join the other angels for the morning hymns of praise to
the Divine.

Argumentative angels are also frequently cited in biblical and post-biblical literature. In *Genesis Rabbah 56:5,* the
angels argued with God over Isaac's sacrifice:

> When the Patriarch Abraham stretched forth his
> hand to take the knife to slay his son, the angels cried
> as it says, "Behold, their valiant ones cry without—
> *'chutzah'"* [Isa. 33:7]. What does *'chutzah'* mean?
> Rabbi Azariah said: "It is unnatural. It is unnatural that
> he should slay his son with his own hand."

A little further on in the Midrash we are told that the
tears of the angels had dissolved the knife that was in
Abraham's hand.

Sometimes angels were seen in rabbinic lore as com-
plainers. Commenting on the verse "in those days when
King Ahasuerus occupied the throne" (Esther 1:2), the
Midrash (Esther Rabbah 1:10) says:

> This was one of the occasions on which the minis-
> tering angels lodged complaints before the Holy One,
> Blessed be He, saying: "Sovereign of the Universe, the
> sanctuary is destroyed and this wretch sits and makes
> carousal." God answered them: "Set 'days' against
> 'days'" [i.e. measure for measure].

In the *Midrash of Genesis 8:10,* we learn about some
confusion on the part of God's ministering angels:

> Rabbi Hoshaya said: When the Holy One created
> Adam, the ministering angels mistook him for a divine
> being, and wished to exclaim 'holy' before him . . .
> What did the Holy One do? He caused sleep to fall

upon him, so that all would know that Adam was indeed a human being.

An interesting discussion related to Lot's angel occurs in the Midrash of *Genesis Rabbah 50:2.* The Bible (Gen. 19:1) tells of two angels that arrived in Sodom in the evening while Lot was sitting in the gate of Sodom. In Genesis 19:5, the townspeople asked Lot to tell them where the men that came to him were. The rabbis in the Midrash were puzzled by the fact that the townspeople referred to the angels as "men" and answered their query in the following way:

In one place you call them angels, whereas earlier they were termed men? Earlier, when the Shechinah was above them, they were men. But as soon as the Shechinah departed from them they assumed the form of angels. Rabbi Levi said: To Abraham, whose strength was great, they looked like men. But to Lot they appeared as angels, because he was weak. Rabbi Chunia said: Before they performed their mission they assumed the style of angels. Rabbi Tanchuma said: They may be compared to a person who received a governorship from the king. Before he reaches the seat of his authority, he goes like an ordinary citizen. Similarly, before they performed their mission, they are called men. Once having performed it, they assumed the style of angels [*Genesis Rabbah 50:2*].

Finally, in the *Midrash Song of Songs Rabbah 1:1,* the rabbis, commenting on the verse from Proverbs 22:29 "seeing a man diligent in his business," attempted to identify the diligent man with the following explanation that includes angelic intervention:

The diligent man refers to Rabbi Chanina. It is told that once, seeing the townspeople taking burnt offerings and peace offerings up to Jerusalem, he exclaimed, "all of them take peace offerings up to Jerusalem and I am unable to take up anything [being that he was so poor]. What am I to do?" Then he went out to the desert land near his town, found a stone, chiselled, polished and painted it, and then he said: "I promise to take this up to Jerusalem." He wanted to employ some carriers, and said to them: "Will you take this stone up to Jerusalem for me?" They said: "Pay us one hundred gold coins and we will take the stone to Jerusalem." He replied: "Where am I going to get a hundred gold coins, or even fifty gold coins to give you?" He could not raise the money and left. Immediately thereafter the Holy One placed in his way five angels in the form of humans. They said to him: "Master, give us five *selahs* and we will take your stone up to Jerusalem, only you must assist us." He was prepared to help them, and immediately they found themselves standing in Jerusalem. He wanted to pay them but could not find them. This incident was reported in the Chamber of Hewn Stone and they said to him: "It would appear that ministering angels brought your stone up to Jerusalem." Then he gave to the sages the sum that he had agreed to pay to the angels.

In sum, all of the previously cited sources bear witness to the fact that angels did play a role in rabbinic tradition. There was however, no attempt to worship angels. In fact, there seems to have been a concerted effort to downgrade the role of angels, as can be attested to by the previously quoted rabbinic statement (Talmud *Chagigah 14a*) that although God creates new angels each day, once they have sung God's praises, they disappear, never to return again.

Although God may on occasion consult them and although angels can argue, complain, debate, and assist humans with good deeds, the angels are ultimately viewed as operating solely under God's power and control. They are subject to God's punishment and can be expelled from their celestial environs. It is true in some cases that angels were superior to human beings, although there were contrary views that supported the claim that a righteous person could achieve an equal status to that of a ministering angel. Such views often included the caveat that such angelic status could be achieved only after death. Indeed, in the Jerusalem Talmud *Shabbat 6:10 8d* there was an opinion that at the end of days, righteous people will rank above the angels and that the angels will learn the divine mysteries from the righteous.

The Prophet Elijah—An Angel of God?

The prophet Elijah, who lived in the ninth century B.C.E. during the reign of King Ahab, has been described as the most romantic and enigmatic figure in the whole range of Jewish history. When Ahab, influenced by his wife Jezebel, had given himself to the worship of the Phoenician god Baal, Elijah's emergence was sudden and most dramatic. He appeared on the scene and predicted a drought as a penalty for the introduction of the Phoenician cult into Israel. Then followed the scene at Mount Carmel, where he demonstrated the miraculous power of God. According to the biblical narrative (1 Kings 18), fire immediately descended from heaven, consuming the burnt sacrifice, and all the people of Israel present fell on their faces chanting "Adonai, He is God, Adonai He is God." At Elijah's command those present attacked and killed the prophets of Baal.

According to 2 Kings 2:1–11, Elijah did not die but was carried to heaven by a chariot and horses of fire. This deep impression left by Elijah's wondrous ministry and his miraculous transportation to heaven in a chariot of fire had already made Elijah a legendary figure in Bible times. According to some mystics, including Moses ben Shem Tov de Leon, Elijah belongs to the angels who advocated the creation of man. He compared Elijah's fate with that of Enoch, the only other biblical personality to have been carried from the earth in an extraordinary manner. The further fate of Elijah and Enoch in heaven was described in vivid detail by Jewish mystics. While Enoch's body was consumed by fire and changed into Metatron, the highest angel, Elijah remained after his travels to heaven in possession of his earthly shape. It is for this reason that he is able to maintain his connection with earthly beings and come back to reappear on earth when necessary.

Many Elijah legends and stories have appeared in Jewish folklore. In many of these Elijah was portrayed as the celestial emissary of God, sent to earth to combat all kinds of social injustice. Elijah was constantly seen as rewarding the poor, who were hospitable, and punishing rich, greedy people. One recurrent theme in the Elijah legends is his ability to ward off the Angel of Death from a young person who is fated to die. This he usually does by advising them to study Torah, an antidote to evil spirits.

Since Elijah did not die and continues to wander the earth, he continues to make appearances at many Jewish life cycle events. For example, Jewish legend holds that Elijah is present at every Jewish circumcision. This is because he bitterly complained (1 Kings 19:10–14) that the Jews would become assimilated since they had forsaken the observance of circumcision. Often considered today as the angel of the covenant (see Mal. 3:1), a special chair called *kisay shel Eliyahu* (the chair of Elijah) is used in

Elijah's honor. The baby is placed upon the chair prior to the surgery, symbolically enabling Elijah to be present in spirit at every circumcision.

According to Jewish tradition, Elijah will come to settle every doubtful case in Judaism shortly before the advent of the Messiah. Elijah's cup of wine, which is placed on the Passover seder table, is linked with a talmudic dispute as to whether four or five glasses of wine are to be used at the seder celebration. Hence the extra cup, known as Elijah's cup, conveys the thought that the question cannot be solved by the authorities of the Talmud and must therefore wait for Elijah's decision.

As the ever-ready defending champion of his people, Elijah has been supposed to rove about the earth testing the hospitality and goodness of men and women. Thus, Elijah's Passover seder cup is more commonly regarded as the glass of wine that is symbolically ready for any fellow Jew who may seek hospitality in response to the invitation extended at the beginning of the Passover seder to the poor and needy.

Since Elijah did not die, and since he is thought to wander the earth looking like his earthly person, there are many who are eager to meet him. Considered the forerunner of the Messiah Himself, he has become an important role model for those who look to engage and become partners in God's work. Many families conclude the *Havdalah* service (the ritual ceremony that concludes the Sabbath) with the singing of the song "Eliyah Ha-Navi"— "Elijah the Prophet." The song expresses the hope that he "come speedily in our days, along with the Messiah, the son of David." Indeed, Elijah, the prophet-angel, continues to show us each week how to live spiritually as humans through his example!

5

ANGELS IN JEWISH LITURGY

It has been said that no religion in the world can be completely understood if its normal daily worship of God is left out of account. This especially applies to Judaism as reflected in the *siddur*, the prayerbook, one of the most popular books in all of Jewish life. If any single volume elicits Jewish values and Jewish thought, it is the prayerbook, which embodies the visions and aspirations, the sorrows and joys, of many generations. The poetic and philosophic creations of both numerous known and unknown authors constitute a considerable part of the prayerbook, with interwoven sections from the Bible, Talmud, and *Zohar*, the book of Jewish mysticism.

The heart of the morning (and evening) services is the *Shema*, Israel's confession of faith. It is, in a sense, the Jewish pledge of allegiance to God's oneness and uniqueness. The *Shema* is preceded by a prayer called the "Yotzer" (meaning "creates"), a thanksgiving prayer to God for the creation of physical and Divine light and the daily renewal of creation. This glorification of God develops the theme that declares God's presence and holiness. Its authorship, in the main, is ascribed to the Jewish mystics of the eighth century. It is not surprising, therefore, that God's Heavenly

Throne was conceived and described by them as being surrounded by angels and all kinds of adoring heavenly bodies. The following are several references to celestial beings as they appear in the daily morning prayer service:

i. In this prayer, called in Hebrew *"titbarach tzurenu,"* God is blessed for having created a myriad of angels, all of whom do His Will, acclaiming God with one voice in unison. This prayer concludes with words taken from the book of Isaiah (6:3), which officially began his ministry as the angels responded with the triad "Holy Holy Holy." To this phrase other angels respond with the words of the prophet Ezekiel (3:12), "Blessed be the Presence of God from God's Place."

> Be blessed, O our Rock, our Sovereign and Redeemer, Creator of holy being . . . Creator of celestial ministering spirits, all of whom stand in the heights of the universe, and with awe proclaim in unison aloud the words of the living and everlasting Sovereign. All of them are beloved, pure and mighty. And all of them in dread and reverence do the will of their Maker. And all of them open their mouths in holiness and purity, with song and psalm, while they bless and praise, glorify and reverence, sanctify and ascribe sovereignty to the Name of the Divine Sovereign, the great, mighty, and awesome Holy One. They all take upon themselves the yoke of the kingdom of heaven one from the other, and give leave one to the other to declare the holiness of their Creator. In tranquil joy of spirit, with purest speech and unique melody, they all respond in unison and exclaim with awe:

> "Holy, Holy, Holy is Adonai Tzeva'ot, the entire earth is filled with God's Presence." [Isa. 6:3] [Note that these words have become the heart of the prayer of sanctification, called the "kedusha"], which is a vital and important part of every prayer service.

And the *Ophanim* (animated angels with wheels), and the holy Chayot [literally, "living creatures"] with a noise of great rushing, upraising themselves toward the Seraphim [fiery angels], thus over against them offer praise and say:

Blessed be the Presence of God from God's Place.

ii. In this prayer, called *"l'El Baruch,"* which directly follows the preceding one, God's angels form a Divine chorus and praise God for creating the lights of the universe. The prayer concludes with a touching Messianic petition: "cause a new light to shine on Zion."

To the blessed God they offer melodious song. To the Sovereign, the living and ever existing God, they utter hymns and make their praises heard. For God alone works mighty deeds and creates new things. God is unique, creating new life, championing justice, sowing righteousness, and reaping victory. God creates healing, and is revered in praises. God is the God of wonders, who in goodness continually renews the creation every day. As it is said: "Praise the Creator of great lights, for God's kindness endures forever. Cause a new light to shine upon Zion and may we all be worthy soon to enjoy its brightness. Blessed are You, O God, Creator of the lights."

iii. In the prayer "Shalom Aleichem," which in some synagogues begins the Friday evening service (others traditionally sing it at their dinner tables on Friday night), ministering angels are welcomed. According to rabbinic legend, God's messengers visit Jewish homes when the Sabbath begins. The following story taken from the talmudic tractate of *Shabbat* is said to have inspired the writing of this prayer:

It was taught: Rabbi Jose son of Rabbi Judah said: Two ministering angels accompany a person on the eve of the Sabbath from the synagogue to the home, one a good angel and one an evil one. When he arrives and finds the lamp burning, the table set and the bed covered with a cloth, the good angel exclaims, "May it be even this way on another Sabbath as well," and the evil angel unwillingly responds "amen." But if not, the evil angel exclaims, "May it be even thus on another Sabbath too," and the good angel unwillingly responds "amen."

Peace be unto you, ministering angels, angels of the
    most High
The Supreme Sovereign of Sovereigns, the Holy
    Blessed One.

Enter in peace, angels of peace, angels of the most High
The Supreme Sovereign of Sovereigns, the Holy
    Blessed One.

Bless me with peace, angels of peace, angels of the
    most High
The Supreme Sovereign of Sovereigns, the Holy
    Blessed One.

Depart in peace, angels of peace, angels of the most
    High
The Supreme Sovereign of Sovereigns, the Holy
    Blessed One.

iv. In the following prayer (taken from the mystical book of the *Zohar,* Vayakhel) which is said as a meditation during the service for taking out the Torah scroll, we are reminded that people are not to put their trust in angels, but rather in God who is the dependable God of truth.

. . . I am the servant of the Holy Blessed One, before whom and before whose glorious Torah I bow down at all times. Not in humans do I put my trust, nor upon any angel do I rely, but upon the God of heaven, who is the God of truth, and whose teaching is truth, and whose prophets are prophets of truth, and who abounds in deeds of goodness and truth . . .

v. One of the teachings of Jewish mystics is that angels are created by the deeds of a person according to the nature of that deed. In the following prayer, called the "Unetaneh Tokef" ("let us declare the utterance of this day"), appearing in the prayerbook called the *Machzor* and recited on the High Holy Days of Rosh HaShanah and Yom Kippur, we are told that even the angels themselves are accountable. With vivid imagery, the author depicts the heavenly scene on Judgment Day, when the *shofar,* the ram's horn, is sounded, but a still small voice to herald the appearance of the Divine Judge is heard. The angels are in terror, for judgment is being decreed against the celestial beings as well as against those who dwell on earth. In God's eyes, no being, however angelic, has perfect purity. The great *shofar* is sounded, and a still small voice is heard. The angels in heaven are dismayed and are seized with fear and trembling as they proclaim, "Behold the Day of Judgment." The celestial beings are to be arraigned in judgment, for "in Your eyes even they are not free from guilt. All who enter the world do You cause to pass before You, one by one, as a flock of sheep . . ."

vi. In the supplication entitled *"Hineni"* ("Behold"), said to have been composed by a humble cantor in the Middle Ages, there is a plea that God will rebuke Satan himself and keep him from blocking the ascent of the prayers. The prayer concludes with a request that it be God's Will that all of the angels that are assigned to prayers will convey the cantor's prayer before God's Throne of Glory.

May it be Your desire, God of Abraham, God of Isaac and God of Jacob, the great, mighty and revered, the

God who is supreme over all . . . that all of the
angels who are assigned to prayers convey my supplication before the Throne of Glory and spread it
before you . . .

vii. In the very beautiful High Holy Day poem, *"Adonai
Melech,"* by Eleazar Kallir (a seventh century poet), the
poet envisioned a vast congregation of fiery celestial beings exclaiming aloud: "God is King, God was King, and
God will be proclaimed King forever." On earth the procla-
mation of the eternal sovereignty of God is, in resounding
manner, echoed by God's earthly hosts—the congregation
of Israel. The prayer is written in the form of an alphabeti-
cal acrostic and beautifully prepares the setting for the
prayer of Sanctification, the *"Kedusha:"*

The heroic sons of a mighty race
Thunderously shout that God is King.
The angels whose figure the lightnings trace
Flame to the world that God was King
And fiery angels whose stature is one with space
Proclaim that God shall be Sovereign forever.

viii. Finally, in the poem entitled *"ameetz hamenusah"*
("mighty and exalted") written by the eleventh century
poet Rabbi Shimon ben Isaac ben Abun of Mayence that is
chanted on the morning of Rosh HaShanah, the exalted
attributes of God are described. The following verses viv-
idly portray aspects of God's heavenly abode:

"Pure in the heavens, wondrous amid God's angels
There is none to compare to God, to do like God . . .

Concealed in clouds, flames leap all around God,
Riding on winged cherubs, lightnings do God's
   Will. . . ."

6

SATAN, FALLEN ANGELS, AND THE ANGEL OF DEATH

Today, Satan is often identified with the devil, Lucifer, or the prince of the demons. This identification is late, and in the Bible Satan is no demon or evil spirit, but belongs to the divine celestial household like the previously described other angelic beings. In its original meaning, the word "satan" means "an adversary who hinders or obstructs." In time the negative or destructive characteristics originally attributed to God were gradually transferred to autonomous demonic beings, and to the extent that these were merely representatives of the principle of evil, Satan was their chief.

Satan in the Bible

In both the Books of Samuel and Kings, the word "satan" is applied to a human adversary and the role of antagonist. For instance, in the book of 2 Samuel 19:22: "David said,

What have I to do with you, you sons of Zeruiah, that you should this day be adversaries ("satan") to me?"

The word "satan" appearing as the name of an actual angel occurs in the Books of Chronicles, Job, and Zechariah. In Zechariah 3, Satan acted as a prosecutor in the celestial court. In the first two chapters of Job, Satan's work included impoverishing Job and rendering him childless. Job, remaining faithful to God, responded in these well known words often heard at the funerals and burials of people of faith: "God has given and God has taken away, blessed be the name of God."

At the next celestial conference, Satan derided Job with these words: "Have you noticed my servant Job? There is no one like him on earth, a blameless and upright man who fears God and avoids evil." Satan, in his further desire to test Job's integrity and faith inflicted Job with severe inflammation (with God's permission, of course). Job's response was, "should we accept only good from God and not accept evil?" (3:9)

Finally, Satan questioned Job's integrity in the latter's absence and suggested that God be tested. He is clearly subordinate to God, and unable to act without God's permission. Although permitted by God to put Job to the test, Satan was always strictly forbidden to touch his person.

Satan in Rabbinic Thought

Rabbinic references to Satan are sporadic, and with few exceptions Satan appears, as in the Bible, as the impersonal force of evil always under God's control. For instance, the *Tosefta Shabbat 17:3* states: "If you see a wicked person setting out on a journey and you wish to go by the same route, anticipate your journey by three days or postpone it for three days, because Satan accompanies the wicked person." Here, Satan is understood as the evil tempter, or in psychological terms, the evil inclination that can and often does take possession of a person.

The same trend is seen in the injunction, "Do not open your mouth to Satan," which appears in the talmudic tractate of *Berachot 9a* and is taught in the name of Rabbi Yose.

The only personification of Satan found in tannatic (the first two centuries c.e.) literature is the story of Rabbi Meir spending three days to bring about a reconciliation between two inveterate quarrelers, upon which Satan complained, "He has drawn me out of my home" (Talmud *Gittin 52a*). Similarly, Rabbi Akiba was tempted by Satan in the form of a woman, but Satan relented.

During the amoraic period, (the third through sixth centuries c.e.) however, Satan became much more prominent in both the Talmud and Midrash. In the Talmud, *Baba Batra 16a*, Satan was identified with the "yetzer hara"—the evil inclination in general—as well as with the Angel of Death. He began to emerge with a more distinctive personality in the talamudic tractate of *Sanhedrin 89b*. There, the Satan of Job who challenged God to put Job to the test of suffering was made to play the same role with Abraham. He accused Abraham that, despite the benefit of being granted a son in his old age, Abraham did not "have one turtle-dove or pigeon to sacrifice before this," and Abraham was thus ordered to sacrifice his beloved son Isaac in order to prove his obedience to God. In this connection an almost sympathetic view was taken of Satan. His purpose in challenging Job's piety, we are told in the Talmud *Baba Batra 16a*, was that God should not forget the greater loyalty to Abraham.

Although we have shown that Satan has appeared as the tempter, he is much more to the fore as the accuser. For instance, in the *Midrash Genesis Rabbah 38:7*, Rabbi Helbo is quoted as saying: "Wherever you find contentment, Satan brings accusations." Furthermore, in the same section, Rabbi Levi is quoted as saying: "Whoever you find eating and drinking, the arch-robber [Satan] cuts his capers" [i.e. does mischief].

In a variety of talmudic and midrashic statements we learn of Satan's responsibility for a variety of different sins: In *Pirke de Rabbi Eliezer 13:1,* we are told that Satan was responsible for all the sins in the Bible, including the fall of humankind; for the people worshipping the golden calf (Talmud *Shabbat 89a*); and for King David's sin with Bat Sheba (Talmud *Sanhedrin 107a*). In the talmudic tractate of *Yoma 67b,* Satan is also associated with the non-Jewish nations in sneering at the *hukkim*—the so-called irrational laws such as the prohibition of eating pig or not mixing linen and wool, thus weakening the religious loyalties of the Jews.

An interesting new reason for sounding the *shofar* on the New Year is provided in the talmudic tractate of *Rosh HaShanah 16b.* There we learn that the purpose of the sounding of the *shofar* is "in order to confuse Satan," but on the Day of Atonement, Yom Kippur, Satan is completely powerless. This is hinted at in the talmudic book of *Yoma 20a,* where we are told that the numerical value of the Hebrew word "satan" is 364. From this the rabbis deduced that there is one day in the year on which Satan is powerless, and that day is Yom Kippur!

Post-Biblical Satan References

Satan is not prominent in the Apocrypha, and where he is mentioned he is hardly personalized but merely symbolizes the forces of anti-God and of evil. A legend that it was Satan who challenged God to put Abraham to the test of sacrificing his beloved Isaac appears in the Book of Jubilees

17:16. There he was called "Mastema," ("Prince of Enmity"), an alternate name for Satan and a quasi-chief of all of the demons. In the Testament of Gad 4:7, the warning is given that "the spirit of hatred works together with Satan through the hastiness of spirit."

In the New Testament Satan emerged as the very personification of the spirit of evil, and unlike in the Judaic sources, has an independent personality. Often called the Antichrist, Satan is the author of all evil (Luke 10:11). In Revelation 12:9, there is a complete description of him, including the following: "that old serpent called the devil and Satan which deceived the whole world. He was cast into the earth and his angels were cast out with him."

He is the personal tempter of Jesus (Matthew 4) and it is this New Testament view of Satan which has entered into popular lore. In the New Testament Book of Revelation 2:9, Jews who would not accept Jesus are referred to as the "synagogue of Satan."

Satan in the Liturgy

There are several references to Satan in the prayerbook. For instance, in the evening prayer "Hashkivenu," which praises God for God's peace and protection, there is a sentence which petitions God to "remove from us the enemy, pestilence, and Satan." Here, Satan is generally understood to be synonymous with the evil impulse, the lower passions which are a hindrance to a person's pursuit of the nobler aims of life. It is against the dominance of this impulse that the Jew continues to pray.

Preceding the daily morning blessing there appears a prayer (originated by Rabbi Judah ha Nasi and appearing in the Talmud *Berachot 16b*) that asks God to spare us from the corrupting Satan. Here again, Satan is generally understood metaphorically to mean the corrupting forces of evil. Such moral hindrances to humans include arrogant people and bad neighbors, which are also cited in the prayer.

It has always been the genius of Judaism to draw on elements of folklore for moral instruction. Among the Jews there persisted vestiges of a primitive belief that the sounding of the *shofar* was intended to expel evil spirits. This may well account for Rabbi Isaac's explanation (Talmud *Rosh HaShanah 16b*) that the purpose of blowing the ram's horn twice during Rosh HaShanah was to confound and confuse Satan. Rabbi Isaac's comment is reflected in the later practice of reciting, before the first series of *shofar* sounds on Rosh HaShanah, six biblical verses which form an acrostic of the words *kera satan* ("destroy Satan"). These verses appear in most High Holy Day prayerbooks and continue to be recited in modern times. It is quite likely that many worshippers today identify the Satan in this acrostic with the evil impulse that can serve as a useful reminder of the all too frequent human tendency of rationalizing sinful conduct into saintly behavior. The words "destroy Satan" can powerfully symbolize the need for all people to wage war against the evil forces within themselves.

A final reference to Satan appears in the stirring prayer called *"Hineni"* appearing in the High Holy Day *Machzor* and chanted on Rosh HaShanah. Tradition ascribes the prayer to a humble cantor in the Middle Ages who, as emissary of the congregation, prayed to God that his prayers would be heard. In the prayer, there is a petition that asks that "Satan be rebuked and not accuse." Here again, the understanding is generally that of a tempter whose evil forces corrupt. Unless these evil forces are sublimated and redirected, they have the power to take full possession of a person and lead that person to the merciless treatment of others.

Fallen Angels

A special category of angels is that of the so-called Fallen Angels, frequently mentioned in post-biblical literature. The concept is common to most Semitic peoples and includes the idea of vanquished gods or demons who rebelled against a chief deity and then reappeared as damned or accursed monsters and demons.

The biblical passage of Genesis 6:14 is often quoted as the basis for all subsequent legends of fallen angels. Here we learn that "Nephilim" appeared on earth when the divine beings cohabited with the daughters of men, who bore them people. According to the commentary of the medieval biblical commentator Rashi, the word "Nephilim" is derived from the verb "nafal" (to fall), and thus the Nephilim are the fallen ones.

The first full account of Fallen Angels appeared in the Pseudepigrapha. Many of the authors of these books attempted to disassociate God from Jewish catastrophe. The use of angels who had gone bad were the perfect device to use for such a purpose, giving rise to the concept of the "Fallen Angel." The earliest report of such angels appeared in the Book of Enoch (chapter 6). The sons of heaven, who belonged to the guardian angels, had passionately desired the beauty of the daughters of men and, in the time of Jared, decided to ascend Mount Hermon to carry out their plans from there. There were two hundred of them, and their leader was Shemhazai, who made them swear an oath to adhere to their purpose, and it was this oath that gave the mountain its name—Hermon. They consorted with the daughters of men, who gave birth to a generation of giants that went about destroying human beings. The Fallen Angels also taught humans to use weapons and other implements that promoted crime. At this point, the four good Archangels, Michael, Uriel, Raphael, and Gabriel, appealed to God and were given the order to punish the Fallen Angels.

The story of Fallen Angels also appears in the Book of Jubilees 4:15 and 5:1ff. There, unlike in the Book of Enoch, the angels were said to have descended to earth to instruct humankind how to order society. When they arrived on earth, they were seduced by the daughters of men.

According to *Midrash Avkir* [1000–1200], a rabbinic commentary on Esther, the leaders of the Fallen Angels, named Shemhazai and Asael (as in the Book of Enoch), heaped scorn upon the sinfulness of the generation of man after the flood. God submitted that if they were on earth, they would also commit sins, and in response to this challenge, they offered to descend to earth. They did so and were immediately seduced by the beauty of the daughters of men. They revealed the secret Name of God to a girl called Ishtar who was able to ascend to heaven and free herself from the hands of Shemhazai. Shemhazai and his compatriots then took wives for themselves who gave birth to two sons, Hiva and Hiya, whose names became the painful cries of suffering people. In this story, as in the Book of Jubilees, the Fallen Angels committed their dastardly deeds after having descended to earth.

Related to the concept of Fallen Angels is another concept found in apocryphal literature, that of the seventy angels that God chose to have power over Israel after the destruction of the First Temple in Jerusalem. These angels, who appeared frequently in the first Book of Enoch, violated God's will and came to be regarded as rebellious angels to whom punishment would be meted out.

The Angel of Death

There are countless legendary and folkloristic tales related to the power of the Angel of Death, a Divine messenger whose task it is to take the soul from the human body. Like all angels, the Angel of Death is, in principle, the personification of a particular Divine act or function. Again, much like the other angels, the Angel of Death over time developed from a particular functionary expression of God to a relatively independent personality with a distinct character of his own.

The Angel of Death is not expressly mentioned in the Hebrew Bible, although there are several passages in which the concept of death seems to become personified. In rabbinic literature the stress seems to be on the positive function of the Angel of Death.

The following talmudic tale (*Avodah Zarah 20a*) attempted to describe the Angel of Death:

> The Angel of Death is said to be full of eyes. When the hour comes for a sick person to die, the Angel of Death positions itself above the head of the sick person with a sword drawn in the angel's hand. On the sword, a drop of gall dangles precariously. When the sick person sees the Angel of Death, the sick person trembles with fear and opens his or her mouth. At that point, the Angel of Death flicks a drop of gall into the sick person's mouth. From the drop, the sick person dies and the face turns green.

In the following talmudic tale (*Baba Batra 11a*), we learn that the giving of *tzedakah* (charity) is one of the many religious obligations that is said to have the power of warding off the Angel of Death:

Benjamin the righteous was in charge of the *tzedakah* box. One day, in the years of a drought, a woman came to him and said, "Rabbi, provide for me." Benjamin answered her, "By God, there is nothing left in the *tzedakah* box." But the woman continued, "If you do not provide for me, a woman and her seven children will die." So he took from his own funds and gave her money.

Only a few days later, Benjamin became sick and was close to his death. The ministering angels came to the Holy Blessed One and spoke on Benjamin's behalf: "Master of the Universe, You have said that 'if one saves a single life, it is as if that person had saved the entire world.' Benjamin the righteous kept alive a woman and her seven children. Should he die in his early years as a result of his charity?" Instantly, his sentence of death was torn up and twenty-two more years were added to his life.

Midrashic tales abound related to the Angel of Death. In the following tale based on *Deuteronomy Rabbah 9:1,* Rabbi Shimon ben Halafta confronted the Angel of Death on his return home from a celebration following the circumcision of a member of his community (It was quite common for the Angel of Death to desire to perform his work at liminal transitional moments in the life cycle, such as a circumcision or even a wedding).

Once Rabbi Shimon ben Halafta went to a feast following a *brit milah* (circumcision). The boy's parents sponsored the banquet and offered their guests seven-year-old wine to drink. They said to their guests, "We will set aside some of this wine for the wedding feast of our son." The celebration continued until midnight.

Rabbi Shimon ben Halafta, who trusted in his power to fight off demons, left the party at midnight in order to return home.

On his way home he encountered the Angel of Death but saw something strange about it. So he said, "Who are you?" The Angel answered, "I am God's messenger." So Rabbi Shimon asked, "Why do you refer to yourself that way?" The Angel replied, "Because of the way people talk. They say, 'We shall do this and this,' and they do not know when they will be called to die. Those people who just celebrated the *brit milah* of their child, their turn will come in thirty days."

Rabbi Shimon said, "Show me my turn." But the Angel of Death replied, "I have no power over you and those like you because the Holy One wants your good deeds and lengthens your and their lives" [*Ecclesiastes Rabbah 3:2*].

Perhaps it is for the reason that death is considered part of life that there are *midrashim*, such as the following one (*Tanchuma Pekudei 3*), that suggests that the angel that accompanies the individual into this world is the same one that accompanies the individual out of the world at death:

When a person's turn to die arrives, the same angel that assisted him at birth comes and says to him, "Do you recognize me?" The person answers, "Yes," and continues "why did you come for me today of all days?" The angel responds, "In order to take you away from this world, for your time to depart has arrived." Instantly the person begins to cry, and her voice is heard from one end of the earth to the other. No creature recognizes his voice except for the rooster.

So the person says to the angel, "You removed me from two worlds and placed me in this world. Why then do you want to take me out of this world?" The angel answers, "Did I not tell you that you were created against your will, born against your will, and will have to give an accounting before the Holy Blessed One against your will?" [*Tanchuma, Pekudei* 3]

Finally, the Angel of Death makes an appearance in the Passover *Haggadah*. In one of the final songs of the *seder* called "Chad Gadya," (one kid) a cast of Israel's oppressors appeared (according to one theory) in the form of symbols: Assyria (the cat), Babylon (the dog), Persia (the stick), Greece (the fire), Rome (the water), the Saracens (the ox), the Crusaders (the slaughterer), and finally the Ottomans, (the Angel of Death). As the curtain came down on the miniature mortality play, retribution was exacted and the Angel of Death was killed by the Holy Blessed One. Thus the Passover *seder* ends on a note of high joy and happiness.

The Angel of Death and Jewish Customs

Belief in the concept of an Angel of Death has also played a role in Jewish custom. For instance, there is a prayer in the form of a blessing for the new Hebrew month that is recited on the Sabbath (at morning services) immediately preceding the new month. The only exception is on the Sabbath before the Hebrew month of Tishri, when the prayer for the new month is not recited. According to Jewish folklore, the prayer was omitted to confuse Satan (or the Angel of Death), since the Angel of Death would be eager to act as the accuser when the children of Israel were judged on Rosh HaShanah. Thus, it became preferable not to remind the angel of the date with the blessing of the new month.

Naming a Jewish child has always been a significant experience. In the case of Jewish names, there is the added significance of Jewish identification. For boys the custom today is to name at the circumcision, and for a female child, to name at a service in the synagogue.

Many years ago it was the custom to name a child immediately upon birth. This custom was changed to the custom of today because it was feared that the name presented a "handle" with which the baby could be reached by the Angel of Death. It was thought that by postponing the naming the Angel of Death could not reach the children during the most fragile first days of life.

A custom that is still carried out today was to change the Hebrew name of a person who was extremely ill and possibly even near death. Accordingly, such a sick person might be given the new name of "Chayim" ("life," for a male) or "Chaya" ("living being," for a female) in order to deceive the Angel of Death through this change in identity.

7

DEMONS, SPIRITS, AND EVIL FORCES

Defending against evil spirits and demons was a concern of all people in the ancient Near East. Considered messengers of the lord of the underworld, demons (in Hebrew, *mazzikim*) were believed to live in the wilderness and near graves. Many of them were spirits of the dead, especially of persons who died a violent death and were not properly laid to rest. Sometimes even sickness was thought to be caused by demonic possession.

Amulets and a variety of incantations were composed with the intention of warding off evil spirits and demons. In one seventh century Phoenician amulet we find the following incantation intended to protect a woman in childbirth:

"Incantations: O Flying One, O goddess, O Sasam. . . . O god, O Strangler of Lambs. The house I enter you shall not enter; the court I rend you shall not tread . . ."

Surrounded by animistic notions of primitive people, the Jews absorbed some of these and developed a variety of legends of their own concerning evil spirits that wield destructive powers over human beings.

Demons in the Bible

In the Book of 1 Samuel 16:14–16, we learn first hand of evil spirits that come to trouble the mind of King Saul:

"Now the spirit of God departed from Saul, and an evil spirit from God terrified him. And Saul's servants said to him: 'Behold now, an evil spirit from God terrifies you. Let our lord now command your servants that are before you, to seek out a man who is skilled on the harp. And it shall be, when the evil spirit from God comes to you, that he shall play with his hand, and you will be cured . . .'"

This story concluded when David played the harp for Saul, who found soothing relief in the music, and the evil spirits departed from his body. What is important to remember in this story is that the evil spirits did not possess an independent will, but rather are sent by God and are fully under God's control and Will.

Demons in the Talmud and Midrash

There are a number of references in the form of legend related to demons, both in the Talmud and midrashic sources. Here is a sampling of them.

i. This rabbinic statement identified the time of day when demons are created: Demons were created at twilight on the eve of the first Sabbath. (Based on *Ethics of the Fathers* 5:6)

ii. In the following midrash we learn that semen that is discharged for purposes other than procreation is said to be utilized by evil spirits to produce their own kind:

Rabbi Jeremiah ben Eleazar said: In all of the years that Adam was under the ban [because he ate of the forbidden fruit], he begot evil spirits—both male and female demons. For it is written, "Adam lived a hundred and thirty years, and begot a son in his own likeness, after his own image" [Gen. 5:3], from which it follows that until that time he did not beget after his own image. [Talmud *Eruvin 18b*]

iii. This Midrash describes some of the physical characteristics of demons:

Our rabbis taught: Six things are said concerning demons. With regard to three, they are like ministering angels. With regard to three others, they are like human beings. They are like ministering angels in that they have wings, they fly from one end of the world to the other, and they can hear what goes on behind the curtain of heaven. They are like human beings in that they eat and drink like humans, they procreate like humans and they die like human beings. [Talmud *Chagigah 16a*]

iv. The Midrash instructs a person who wishes to become aware of the existence of demons:

One who desires to become aware of demons' existence should take carefully sifted ashes and sprinkle them in his bed. In the morning, he will notice something like the tracks of a cock. One who wishes to see them should take the afterbirth of a black cat that is the offspring of a black cat and a firstborn of a firstborn. One should parch the afterbirth in fire, grind it into powder, and put a generous pinch of the mixture into his eyes. Then one will see the demons. [Talmud *Berachot 6a*]

v. This statement describes the demon of bitter destruction:

Rabbi Huna said in the name of Rabbi Yose: The demon of bitter destruction is covered with scales and hair and shines with his one eye. That eye is in the middle of his chest. He is powerless when it is cool in the shade and hot in the sun, but only when it is hot in both shade and sun. He rolls like a ball and from the seventeenth of Tammuz until the Ninth of Av, he has power after ten o'clock in the morning and until three o'clock in the afternoon. Any person who sees this demon falls on his face and dies. [*Midrash, Numbers Rabbah 12:3*]

vi. The following rabbinic tale tells of the efficacy of prayer in working to eradicate a demon:

It once occurred that a certain demon haunted Abaye's house of study. Even though during the day people entered in prayers, they still were harmed. Abaye then said to his students: "Let no one offer lodging to Rabbi Acha [so that he would be forced to spend the night in Abaye's house of study]. Perhaps through his merit a miracle will take place."

Rabbi Acha went to the house of study where he did spend the night. The demon appeared to him as a seven-headed dragon. Each time, Rabbi Acha fell to his knees in prayer, and one of the demon's heads fell off. That next day, Rabbi Acha chided them: "If a miracle had not occurred, you would have put my life in danger." [Talmud *Kiddushin 29b*]

vii. This statement, a compendium of a variety of rabbinic sources, cites the places in which demons dwell and sport:

Their sporting places are caper bushes and spearworts, where they dwell in groups of sixty; nut trees, where they form in groups of nine; shady spots on moonlight nights, especially the roofs of houses, under gutters, or near ruins; cemeteries and toilets (there is a special demon of the privey known in Hebrew as *shayd shel bet ba-kissay*); water, oil and bread crumbs cast on the ground; and there are persons and things coming near them. [Talmud *Pesachim 3b; Berachot 3a, 62b; Shabbat 67a; Gittin 70a; Chullin 105; Sanhedrin 65b*]

viii. The following statement describes the most dangerous nights for demons:

Especially dangerous are the evenings of Wednesday and of the Sabbath, for then Agrat bat Machlat, the dancing roof demon (Yalkut Chadash, Keshafim 56) haunts the air with the train of eighteen myriads of messengers of destruction, every one of whom has the power of doing harm [See Talmud *Pesachim 112b*]. On those nights one would not drink water except out of white vessels and after having recited Psalm 29:3–9 (in it the "voice of God" is mentioned seven times) or other magical formulas. [Talmud *Pesachim 3a*]

ix. Although demons are usually destructive spirits, in some cases they can be helpful, saving forces:

The saint Abba Jose of Zaintor saved his town from harm, when informed by a water demon living nearby that a dangerous fellow demon made his habitation there, by causing the inhabitants to go down to the edge of the water at dawn, equipped with iron rods and spits, and beat the intruder to death. The blood marked the spot where he was called. [See *Midrash Leviticus Rabbah 24*]

x. In the following reference we learn that some of the Babylonian rabbinic authorities employed demons as friendly spirits, even referring to them on a first name basis: "Rabbi Joseph said, 'The demon Joseph told me that Ashmadai, the king of the demons, is appointed over all pairs and a king is not designated a harmful spirit'" (Talmud *Pesachim 106a*).

xi. Demons were generally creators of harm, often causing disease. In the following passage we learn of the demon that causes blindness as well as the antidote against it:

Our rabbis taught: A person should not drink water from rivers or pools at night, and if one drinks, his blood is on his own head because of the danger. What is the danger? The danger of "shabriri" (i.e. demon of blindness). But if he is thirsty, what is the remedy? If a person is with him he should say to him, "So-and-so the son of so-and-so, I am thirsty for water." But if not, let him say to himself, "O so-and-so, my mother told me, 'Beware of shabriri: Shabriri, briri, riri, iri ri' [This is an incantation against the blindness demon that resembles an 'abracadabra' amulet, in which each succeeding line is reduced by one letter], I am thirsty for water in a white glass." [Talmud *Pesachim 112a*]

xii. In this selection we learn of the demon that brings the disease of the croup to children:

When Rabbi Huna was in possession of some medi-
cament, he would take a pitcherful of it, hang it on the
doorpost and say: "Whoever wishes to have some, let
that person come and take it." Some report that he
knew of a medicine against a disease called *shibta*
(often understood to mean a female demon who
would bring the croup disease to those who did not
wash their hands in the morning), and he would place
it on a jug of water, hang the latter outside and say:
"Any person who needs it, let that person come and
use it to avoid danger." [Talmud *Taanit 20b*]

xiii. In this talmudic statement we learn of the fear of
demons at night: "It is forbidden for one person to greet
another at night for fear that person might be a demon"
(Talmud *Megillah 3a*).

Demons in Jewish Mysticism

Jewish mystics made use of many of the talmudic and midrashic motifs and developed their particular system of demonology, based on the notion that there is a realm of
darkness and evil in God's world which even God cannot
reach. This dark world is filled with evil spirits, with Lilith
linked to her husband Samael (often identified as the Angel
of Death himself). Castillian kabbalists linked the existence
of demons themselves with the last grade of the powers of
the left-side emanation *sitra achra* which corresponds with
its ten *sefirot* of evil to the ten holy *Sefirot*. This contrasts
with the *Zohar,* the book of Jewish mysticism, which follows the talmudic legend that connected the origin of demons in sexual intercourse between humans and demonic
powers. This sexual element in the relationship of humans
and demons played a leading role in the demonology of the

Zohar. In later mystical writings it was explained that demons born to humans create illegitimate sons, called *banim shovavim* ("mischievous sons"). At death, these sons are prone to come to accompany the dead person and to claim their inheritance share. They may also attempt to injure the legitimate children. This notion has given rise to a cemetery custom of circling the dead in order to repulse the demons.

Specific Demons

In the Bible foreign gods are called "shedim," often rendered "demons" in translation. For instance, in Psalm 106:37 we are told that the people "sacrificed their sons and daughters to the demons." This greatly angered God, causing Him to allow the enemies of the Israelites to defeat and oppress them.

Some demons are specifically mentioned by name and have a somewhat illustrious history in post-biblical literature. Here is a summary of some of the more well-known specific demons in the world of Jewish demonology:

1. *Resheph:* Resheph was the Canaanite netherworld god of pestilence. While not specifically mentioned in the Bible as a god, the name does appear in the Bible. In both Deuteronomy 32:24 and Habakkuk 3:5, "resheph" appears as a synonym for pestilence.

2. *Azazel:* The Israelite biblical conception of demons resembled in a number of ways the conception of demons in other cultures. For example, we learn that demons lived in deserts. In the annual ritual ceremony of purification in the ancient sanctuary, Aaron was told to offer two goats, one to God and the other for Azazel, and the goat was to be sent into the wilderness (Lev. 16:1–10). Many Bible critics,

including Nachmonides and Ibn Ezra, shared the view that "Azazel" is the name of a demon in the wilderness.

3. *Dever:* In Psalm 91:5–6, we are told the following: "You need not fear the terror ("pachad") of night, the arrow ("chetz") that flights by day. The pestilence ("dever") that prowls in the dark, the scourge ("ketev") that stalks at noon." Some Bible commentators have associated the Hebrew word "dever" with the demon of pestilence. Others have identified all of the Hebrew words in quotations above as quite likely being associated with the names of demons.

4. *Agrat bat Machlat:* This female demon seems to be the mistress of the sorceresses who communicated magic secrets to Amemar (see Talmud *Pesachim 110a and 112b*).

5. *Lilith:*

i. In the Bible and Talmud: One female demon that is assigned a major central position in Jewish demonology is that of Lilith. Today, there is even a popular Jewish feminist magazine named after her! She is often traced to Babylonian demonology, which identified similar male and female spirits—Lilu and Lilitur.

The first and only biblical reference to Lilith is in the Book of Isaiah 34:14, where she was listed as one of the spirits that will lay waste to the land on the day of vengeance:

> "Wildcats will meet hyenas,
> And the satyr shall cry to his fellow
> Yea, Lilith shall repose there
> And shall find her a place of rest."

Lilith is mentioned several times in the Talmud in the following contexts. In the Talmud *Eruvin 100b,* she appears as a female demon with a woman's face, long hair and wings. We learn in the talmudic tractate of *Shabbat 151b* that, according to Rabbi Chanina, a person sleeping in a house alone is liable to be seized by Lilith. In the Talmud *Baba Batra 73a,* we are told that the demon Hormin is one of Lilith's sons.

A female demon who is known by tens of thousands of names and moves about the world at night, visiting women in childbirth with the intent of strangling their newborn children, is mentioned in the third century Greek Testament of Solomon, a book of the Pseudepigrapha. Here she is called Obizoth, and it is related that one of the mystical names of the guardian angel Raphael inscribed on an amulet will prevent her from doing any serious damage or inflicting injury upon another.

ii. Lilith in the Midrash: There are numerous rabbinic legends regarding Lilith. For instance, in the *Alphabet of Ben Sira,* a tenth century work, a legend appeared that attempted to explain the widespread custom of writing amulets against Lilith. In this work she was identified with the "first Eve," who was created from the earth at the same time as Adam, and who, unwilling to forgo her equality, disputed with him the manner of their intercourse. Pronouncing God's Name, she flew off into the air. Adam then requested that God send three angels, Snwy, Snsnwy, and Smnglf, after her. Locating her at the Red Sea, the angels threatened that if she did not return, one hundred of her sons would die every day. She refused, stating that the very nature of her existence was to harm newborn infants. However, she was forced to swear that whenever she saw the image of those angels in an amulet, she would lose her power over the infant.

In the *Midrash of Numbers Rabbah (end of chapter 16)*, we are told that Lilith turned upon her own children when she found no children born. This particular motif is said to relate her to the Babylonian Lamashtu.

iii. Lilith in Kabbalah: In mystical tradition, Lilith has two basic roles: one who strangles children and one who seduces men, resulting in nocturnal emissions. Through these emissions she bears a never-ending number of demonic children. She is numbered among the four mothers of the demons, the others being Agrat, Machalath, and Naamah. In addition, she became the permanent partner of Samael, queen of the realm of the evil forces. In this world of evil she is the mother of the unholy folk, ruling over all that is impure.

Lilith has also been identified with the Queen of Sheba, based on a Jewish and Arab myth that the Queen of Sheba was actually a jinn, half human and half demon. Although no one knows for sure the exact reason for this connection, there is a fair amount of interesting conjecture. It may well be related to the fact that in the first chapter of the Book of Job 1:15, we are told that Job's seven sons and three daughters were slain by a force from Sheba. The Targum, the Aramaic translation of the Hebrew Bible, understands Lilith as the instigating force that caused the destruction of Job's children. In Ashkenazic folklore she is depicted as a snatcher of children, a demonic witch, and a seductive dancer.

In the Kabbalah, (*Zohar* Ra'aya Meheimna III 227b), influenced by astrology, Lilith is related to the planet Saturn and all those of a melancholy disposition—of a "black humor"—are her sons. From the sixteenth century it was believed that if a baby laughed in its sleep that it was an indication that Lilith was playing with him, and it was thus advisable to tap him on the nose to avert danger.

It gradually became quite common to protect women who were giving birth from Lilith's great power by placing amulets over the bed or on all four walls of the room. According to *Shimmush Tehillim,* a book dating from the Geonic period, amulets written for women who used to lose their children customarily included Psalm 126 (later replaced by Psalm 121) and the names of the three angels Sanvei, Sansanavei, and Samangalaf.

6. *Asmodeus* (*Ashmedai*): All of the demons were believed to be under the dominion of a chief called Asmodeus. Said to be derived from the Persian "aesmadiv" ("spirit of anger"), Asmodeus is described as king of the demons in the Talmud *Pesachim 110a*: "Rabbi Joseph said: 'The demon Joseph told me that Ashmedai the king of the demons is appointed over all pairs.'"

Interestingly, the Talmud in the main does not describe Asmodeus as only an evildoer. In the well known talmudic account in the tractate of *Gittin 68a, b,* although Asmodeus usurped the throne of King Solomon, he provided the king with the *shamir,* a magical worm whose touch split rocks, enabling Solomon's workers to hew stones for the Temple in Jerusalem without the use of prohibited tools of iron.

Asmodeus is also described in the Talmud *Gittin 8a* as "rising every day from his dwelling place on the mountain to the firmament," where he "studies in the Academy on High." As a result of this daily practice, he gains knowledge of the fate of human beings which often causes him to act in an enigmatic fashion. For example, while on his way to Solomon, Asmodeus wept upon seeing a wedding party, later explaining that the bridegroom had only a small amount of time to live. Similarly, on the same journey, he set a drunkard on the right path in order that he might have a share in the world to come.

Asmodeus first appeared in the apocryphal Book of Tobit 3:8–17 which described how, in a fit of jealousy, he slaughtered the successive husbands of a young girl. He was later portrayed as a lawbreaker and the creator of discord between husband and wife in the first century work The Testament of Solomon. Throughout later legendary works, he was for the most part portrayed as mischievous and promiscuous, an almost degraded humorous hero.

Various speculations have been made on the demise of the king of the demons. There is a tradition that he died a martyr's death with the Jews of Mainz in 1096. Another mystical viewpoint is that Asmodeus is merely the title of the office of the king of the demons, just as Pharaoh is the title of the office of the king of Egypt, and that every king of the demons is called Asmodeus. (The word Asmodeus, in *gematriah*, has the same numerical equivalent as that of Pharaoh!)

How to Avoid Demons

There have been many activities devised through the ages by which to eradicate and avoid the demons. The observance of the Law was clearly one of the best prophylactics against demons. Wearing *tefillin* (phylacteries), affixing a *mezuzah* to one's doorpost, and the putting on of *tzizit* (prayer shawl fringes) while directly observing the Law were regarded by the rabbis as safeguards against all evil powers (see Talmud *Berachot 5a*). The *Midrash Numbers Rabbah 9:5* mentions that a priest's blessing protects against evil forces, while the *Midrash Exodus Rabbah 32* presents the idea that "when a person performs one *mitzvah,* the Holy Blessed One gives that person one angel to guard him. . . ," and that "when a person performs two *mitzvot,* God gives that person two angels to guard him."

The Mishneh, *Shabbat 6:2 and Shekalim 3:2,* mentions that amulets were worn for the curative power they were believed to possess. A protective force was attributed to inscribed amulets, which were often folded with mystical writings in them in addition to magical symbols. The construction of amulets and magical incantations as devices to help ward off evil spirits has a fascinating literature. Many amulets included various combinations and permutations of the letters of different names of God. Names of angels were also used as well. Pictures depicted on various amulets often included the star of David, the *menorah,* and an outstretched hand. Three biblical verses (Ex. 14:19–21) were believed to have strong mystical significance, because each of them consists of seventy-two letters of one of the mysterious names of God. Hence, these verses were assumed to represent the ineffable Divine Name. They were inserted in the amulets in varied forms as an appeal to God for protection.

The mystical word "abracadabra," derived from the Aramaic tongue, was often used as a formula of incantation against fever or inflammation. Medieval patients were advised to wear this magic word, written in the following manner on an amulet, in the belief that it would ward off and cure diseases:

A B R A C A D A B R A

A B R A C A D A B R

A B R A C A D A B

A B R A C A D A

A B R A C A D

A B R A C A

A B R A C

A B R A

A B R

A B

A

A similar idea is quoted in the Talmud *Pesachim 112a* to the effect that as an incantation against the evil force of blindness ("shabriri") a person should say: "My mother has told me to beware of shabriri: shabriri, briri, riri, iri, ri."

Other devices for warding off demons included the following: carrying lit torches at night; buying them off with gifts and bribes; deceiving them using disguises; piety and having a good family name; biblical readings (especially Psalm 91); blowing the ram's horn; onions, garlic, leeks, and spices; the colors red and blue; sweet things; keeping a knife on hand; rinsing with running water; keeping one's house clean and tidy; and spitting three times.

It is likely that some of the customs at Jewish life cycle events are protective measures against demons, who enjoy wreaking havoc at transitional moments in the lives of humans. Here is a brief summary of these folk customs:

1. *Circumcision:*

i. Placing red ribbons and garlic on a baby boy's crib prior to his circumcision to ward off evil spirits.

ii. Placing a knife under the pillow of the mother the night before the circumcision to protect her from evil spirits.

iii. During a difficult labor, placing a Torah belt around the belly of the mother.

iv. Placing candy under the bed of the new mother to draw the attention of evil spirits away from her and the baby.

v. In Eastern Europe, throwing sugar, raisins, and cake into the baby's cradle before the child was placed in it.

vi. Naming the baby after a strong animal such as a lion ("Aryeh") or bear ("Dov") could transfer the strength of the animal to the infant and frighten away the evil spirits.

vii. Not disclosing the name of the newborn before the circumcision was meant to prevent the evil spirits from harming it, since they could not identify it.

viii. At the celebration after the birth of a male child, one was to serve beans and peas, which were believed to effectively ward off evil demons and spirits.

2. *Wedding:*

i. Demons are notorious for their jealousy of bride-grooms, and the latter were believed to be in grave danger until their brides walked three or seven times around them under the bridal canopy. Here, the protective power of the circle was frequently used in magical practice, since it allowed the practitioner the safety of a protected space from which he could invoke various spirits to carry out his wishes. Drawing a circle around someone who was be-lieved to be in mortal danger was thought to protect him or her from the demonic attack.

ii. Fifteenth century bridegrooms were described as wearing mourning garb and spreading ashes upon them-selves in order to fool the evil forces. Among Oriental Jews, the act of deception took the form of painting the faces of both bride and groom to disguise their real identities.

iii. The noise from the breaking of the glass at the end of every Jewish wedding ceremony was said to protect against the forces of evil spirits and demons.

iv. Candles were often lit during wedding processionals and sometimes even carried by those in the wedding party in order to frighten away the evil spirits.

v. The custom of the fast of the bride and bridegroom on the day of their wedding has been known to fool the evil spirits into thinking that it is a day of mourning rather than one of ultimate joy.

vi. Breaking a dish when announcing the engagement of a couple was said to frighten away evil spirits.

vii. Tuesday was thought to be an auspicious day for a wedding because, in the creation story in the Book of Genesis, God said of the third day that "it was good" two times, while of the other days the phrase "it was good" was only mentioned once.

3. *Death:*

i. Making seven stops before a casket was laid into the ground at a cemetery was said to protect against evil spirits.

ii. Pouring out household water from the house of a mourner was done so that the evil spirits could not cross the water. The intention was to insure that the soul did not remain trapped inside the home.

iii. Watching a dead body (before burial) while reading Psalms was considered a strong antidote to evil spirits.

iv. Some people followed the custom after leaving a cemetery of plucking blades of grass and throwing them behind their backs, thus repelling the evil spirits that lurked behind.

The Dybbuk

There has been a popular belief in Jewish folklore that suggests the possibility of an evil spirit having the capability of entering a living person, causing that person to take on personality traits of the evil spirit. This evil spirit is called a "dybbuk," meaning "a clinging soul." The term "dybbuk" itself did not appear in early rabbinic literature and was a later one that was introduced into seventeenth century literature.

The earliest example of demonic possession in Jewish tradition was the "evil spirit" that overtook King Saul in 1 Samuel 16:14ff, causing him to fly into a wild rage with no apparent provocation. King Saul himself sought out the spirit of the dead prophet Samuel (1 Sam. 28:3ff). The Talmud relates that, to help Rabbi Shimon bar Yochai have anti-Jewish decrees annulled, a demon entered the body of the Emperor's daughter. Upon Rabbi Shimon's command, the demon left. Thus was Rabbi Shimon ingratiated to the Emperor Vespasian, who then rescinded the edict.

The notion of a foreign spirit entering and gaining control of a human body is found in both Jewish and Christian literature of the talmudic age, particularly in the New Testament. It was not, however, a common phenomenon, and consequently, we have few texts or manuals giving instruction in expelling them. Though medieval literature, especially the works on *Hasidei Askhenaz,* is rife with practical advice on avoiding and appeasing the demons, it seems that people who lived then were not troubled by actual possessions. It was not until the sixteenth century that the phenomenon of possession began to grow extremely popular, especially in the school of Isaac Luria and his chief disciple Chayim Vital.

At first the dybbuk was considered to be a demonic spirit that entered into the body of a sick person. For the past few centuries, it is more likely that the dybbuk was understood to mean the spirit of a sinner who had died and not rested peacefully. Such spirits that take possession of a human body and completely control its personality can be expelled only by the most powerful of exorcisms.

Sephardic kabbalists differentiated between possession by a wandering soul of some deceased Jew (an evil spirit) and possession by a demon. Different rites of expulsion were given for each, and demons, unlike evil spirits, were said to be distinguished by these criteria: a demon would coerce a person, make a person twitch hands and feet, and spit up white foam. Evil spirits, on the other hand, would cause a person to feel pain and at will could constrict the heart, causing a person to faint.

Not all dybbuks were evil possessors in the strictest sense. Rabbi Chayim Vital recounted the story of a young woman possessed of a spirit, in which a male voice speaking through her claimed to be the spirit of a God-fearing sage who was sent out from the Garden of Eden to perform a short mission to expiate for a minor transgression. The mission was intended to warn Rabbi Vital that the Damascan Jews were in extreme danger unless they could be convinced to repent of their sins.

As folktales about various dybbuks began to proliferate, some found their way into literary expression. S. Ansky, author and folklorist of the early twentieth century, was the author of the most famous dybbuk story, his Yiddish play *Der Dybbuk*. It was later translated into Hebrew by Chayim Nachman Bialik and performed by the Israeli theater troupe Habimah in Moscow, Tel Aviv, and New York. In 1938 a film of the play by a Polish–Yiddish company was produced. In the story, Chanan, a young Yeshiva student, falls in love with Leah, daughter of the wealthy merchant Reb Sender. Chanan wants to marry her, but the girl's father arranges for her to marry a wealthier person. Chanan, in a desperate attempt to become wealthy, turns to kabbalistic magic, which drives him to madness and ultimately to his death. Leah begins to frequent the cemetery where Chanan is buried, and on the eve of her wedding becomes possessed by Chanan's soul. Her father then consults with a rebbe, who then dreams of a meeting with the spirit of Chanan's father. The father tells him that Sender and he were once close friends that had pledged their yet unborn children in marriage if they should happen to be a boy and a girl. Chanan's father dies, and Sender forgets his vow. Chanan's father now demands justice from a rabbinical court, which rules that lives of unborn cannot be pledged, and that Sender must now do penance. An exorcism is performed, and the dybbuk (i.e. Chanan's spirit) eventually withdraws from Leah's body. Leah's soul also departs to join her dead lover in eternal wandering.

Rituals for Jewish Exorcism

There has been much to do lately with demons, spirits, and exorcisms, partly due to William Blatty's best-selling novel, *The Exorcist,* and the motion picture of the same name. By the time that Chayim Vital moved to Damascus from the holy city of Safed in the late fifteenth century, he began to associate himself with a small group of mystics favoring resort to alchemy, chants, and magical incantations, often borrowed from non-Jewish sources. Exorcisms in this style became popular then, and many involved elaborate rituals including smoke and burning sulphur, writing sacred names on parchment and hanging them around the neck of the host's body, and garbled Latin invocation. A small number of exorcisms have been preserved in post-kabbalistic literature, including: Turino, 1672 ("Egeret Ramaz"); Nicholsberg, 1696 (Moshe ben Menachem, "Sera HaKodesh"); and Jerusalem, 1904 (S. R. Mizrachi, "Ma'aseh haruach shel Norah").

Here is a sample formula for exorcising an evil spirit by Rabbi Chayim Vital:

Here is a *yichud* which my teacher (Luria) taught me, to exorcise an evil spirit (God forbid!); for there are times when the spirit of some evil man, which cannot enter paradise because of its sins, wanders about the world, and sometimes enters the body of some man or woman, and makes him fall down, and this is called epilepsy (*cholay hanofel*). And by means of this *yichud,* his (i.e. the sinner's soul) is lifted a bit, and it can leave the man's body. And these are the details, which I myself have tried: I would take the arm of the man, and put my hand on his pulse of the right or left hand (for that is the garment of the spirit, and it is clothed therein). And I direct my mind to the spirit clothed in the pulse, that by the power of the *yichud* it should leave.

While I am still holding the man's arm at the pulse, I say this verse forwards and backwards. And I concentrate on the holy names which come from it [e.g. those from the numerical equivalent of each word, and from the initial letters of each word, and from the last letter of each word, as is known]. And during this [i.e. the concentration on the names] I direct my mind that the spirit should exit the body. And then the spirit speaks to you from the body, and tells you anything you might ask, and you should command him to exit.

Sometimes one must blow the *shofar* near his ear, and meditate on the name "kera satan," and also on its reverse, in *atbash* "dezak bant."

And know, that this spirit never comes alone, but a devil supports it, and leads him wandering to complete the recompense for its sins. And he can do nothing without the permission of this devil, for God has appointed him guard over it, as it is written in the *Zohar* [*Bo, 41b*]: "The evil inclination rules the wicked."

Sometimes the spirit leaves the body, and the devil remains alone to guard the place. Therefore, the roaming spirit does not constantly inhabit the afflicted boy, for it sometimes must leave at appointed times to receive its punishment. Nonetheless, the appointed devil remains to guard the place, and the afflicted person is never healed from his illness, until both of them exit.

And now I shall copy the text of the Meditation.

א) הפקד עליו רשע ושטן יעמד על ימינו
ב) ימינו על יעמד ושטן רשע עליו הפקד
ג) ונימי לע דמעי נטשו עשר וילע דקפה

The order of these vowels follows the order of the vowels of the *Sefirot,* as it is recorded in *Tikkune Zohar* [*TZ, 70 p. 129*]. Know, that these seven words, when inverted in the above order, are divine names. And I am doubtful if one should meditate on these names when one recites the verse backwards, or perhaps he should read it forwards and backwards, and then meditate on these names: this latter seems more correct.

ד) סנזגיאל מטטרון נורטסמ יננגפל (אתב"ש)

ה) ייה יהו יהוה יוד יוד הא יוד הא ואו יוד הא ואו הא

ו) יואחצצבירון

ז) קרע שטן ילי מכמ

You should concentrate, that it should leave by the power of all these names. And if he does not exit, repeat the verse, and meditate on all the above names, and after each time say: Leave! Leave! Quickly. Know, that the most important thing is that you should be strong of heart, without any fear; do not have a soft heart, for if you do he will be strengthened and will not listen to you.

You must also command him not to leave the body from any place except the spot between the nail and flesh of the big toe, so as not to injure the body.

Also, command him by the force of these names which you have meditated, and with excommunication חרם and נדן that he may not injure or enter the body of any other Jew.

Know, that when it speaks, the man's body remains mute as a stone, and the spirit's voice comes from the mouth, without any moving of the lips, as a small, child-like voice. Also, when the voice comes up from the body to the mouth to speak, the form of some round gland [לוז] ascends through the neck to the skin of the neck, and again when it descends to the big toe.

Know, furthermore, that when you ask it who it is and what is its name, it will lie and give another name, either to mock you, or so that your command would not take effect (i.e. when you adjure it by name). Therefore, you must adjure him with threats of excommunication, and the power of the Names, not to lie at all, but to tell you who he is with all truth. It is necessary to perform this deed with ritual purity, and ritual immersions, and with holiness and excessive concentration.

To force a demon to leave:

Say the following incantation thirty times in his left ear and thirty times in his right ear, and do not pause between them, and he will leave. Also, if you write it on parchment and hang it around his neck, the demon will leave, or at least it will descend to the foot and will not be able to rise. Seeing that it can no longer ascend, it will leave by itself after a few days. And here is the incantation: Altinum, Sabtinum, Tanrikum, Sabtinotis, Kintiel, Yah, Hai-Hu, Amen, Amen; Kirlorah, Akhsah, Kalba, Da, v'Reshith, Amen, Amen, Tar. [H. Vital, "Sha'ar Ruach HaKodesh" (Tel Aviv, 1963) pg. 88ff]

The Evil Eye

The terms *ayin hara* and *ayn hara* essentially denote envy, jealousy, and greed. In the Hebrew Bible we are told not to dine with a person who is stingy (*ayn ra*) and not to desire that person's delicacies. Opposed to the grudging person is the generous person (*tov ayin*) in Proverbs 22:9. In the *Ethics of the Fathers* 2:13–14, we are told that a good eye (*ayin tovah*), or generosity, is the best quality to which a person should cling, and that an evil eye (*ayn hara*) is the worst quality, which a person ought to shun.

Over the course of time, it became a widespread belief that an envious or begrudging glance of the eye could work evil upon the person to whom it was directed. According to a statement from the Talmud, *Baba Metzia 107b,* "Ninety-nine out of a hundred die of an evil eye."

There are numerous midrashic references to the evil eye. In *Genesis Rabbah 45:5–6,* we learn that Rabbi Hoshaya believed that the evil eye took possession of Hagar, causing her to miscarry. Later in *Genesis Rabbah 53:13,* we are told that Sarah cast an evil eye upon Ishmael, causing him to be seized with feverish pains. Rabbi Jose, the son of Rabbi Chanina, stated in *Genesis Rabbah 56:11* that, after Abraham substituted a ram for sacrificial purposes rather than his son Isaac, he sent Isaac home at night, fearing the evil eye.

In the *Midrash of Leviticus Rabbah 17:3,* there is a litany of ten things that are mentioned in connection with causing the dreaded biblical disease of leprosy. The last of the list is the evil eye! Later, in the *Midrash of Leviticus Rabbah 26:7,* we are told that if a man went to a feast, he did not take his children with him, fearing the evil eye.

In the *Midrash of Numbers Rabbah 12:4,* we learn that, when a king was about to give his daughter in marriage, he gave her an amulet and said to her: "Keep the amulet upon you so that the evil eye may have no power over you any more."

In the *Midrash of Deuteronomy Rabbah 1:25,* commenting on the phrase "For I have delivered them into your hand," we are told that Og, King of Bashan, began to cast an evil eye upon the Israelites. God interceded and said to him: "Why do you cast your evil eye upon My children? May your eye run out; you are destined to fall by their hand."

Finally, the evil eye was said to have caused the breaking of the first tablets of the Law in the *Midrash of Numbers Rabbah 12:4* and the death of Daniel's three companions (Chananiah, Mishael, and Azariah) in the Talmud *Sanhedrin 93a*.

The power of the evil eye was not only confined to evildoers. Sometimes, rabbinic heroes were able to use the power of the eye for benevolent purposes. For instance, Rabbi Shimon ben Yochai is described transforming an evil person into a "heap of bones" by means of his amazing ability (Talmud *Shabbat 34a*). With the glance of an eye, Rabbi Yochanan was able to kill a man who uttered malicious statements about Jerusalem (Talmud *Baba Batra 75a*).

The *Code of Jewish Law* (chapter 23, Ganzfried's Abridged Version), states that two brothers, whether of one father or of one mother, could not be called up to the Torah in succession; nor could a father and son, or grandson, be called up in succession, because of the evil eye.

Finally, the *Midrash Tanchuma 66* states that "a person will call his handsome son "Ethiop" (in Hebrew, *kushee*) in order to avoid casting the evil eye upon him.

How to Avoid the Evil Eye

Many folk beliefs and customs are evident, even today, that work to ameliorate the deleterious effects of the evil eye. Measures taken to avert the evil eye come in two forms. In the preventative, the belief exists that the evil eye is activated by arousing the jealousy of the so-called endowed people. This measure calls for preventive measures of self-restraint, such as the avoidance of an expression of praise for a handsome newborn, one who is especially susceptible to the evil eye. The other form is counteractive, meaning that once the evil eye has been activated and the threat of danger is imminent, there is no need for a preventative measure, but rather an immediate confrontation using countermagic, which works to deceive or ultimately defeat the evil eye.

Here is a cross-section of some of the ways of averting the evil eye:

Preventative Measures

i. Do not spread a costly garment over the bed when guests are visiting a house, as "it will be burned by the eye of the guests" (Talmud *Baba Metzia 30a*).

ii. Break precious glass at a wedding to avert the evil eye.

iii. Veil your beauty and do not exhibit your riches, both of which are susceptible to the evil eye.

iv. Tie a red band around the wrist or neck of a newborn to avert the evil eye.

v. Wear a *chamsa* (from the Arabic word for "five," an amulet that looks like a hand and often contains the evil eye in its center) around your neck for continuous protection from the evil eye.

vi. Use an outstretched arm to try to avert the evil eye.

vii. Use a mirror or a specific color (red or blue) to continuously reflect the potential glance of the evil eye.

viii. Avoid double weddings in one household!

ix. Never use the term "evil eye" in conversation. Instead, use the term "good eye" as a euphemism in its place.

x. Never count people using "one, two, three," etc., since numbering people creates a special susceptibility to the evil eye. If you need to count people, count "not one," "not two," and so on.

xi. If taking your child to school for his or her first time, screen your child with your cloak.

xii. Never mention the date of birth or the exact age of a person.

xiii. Wear an amulet inscribed with different names of God and good angels. You may also choose a protective verse, such as Genesis 49:22, believed to be a potent antidote to the evil eye: "Joseph is a fruitful vine, a fruitful vine by a fountain." (Note: The Hebrew word for "vine" (*ayin*) is also the Hebrew word for "eye.")

xiv. Put a piece of Passover *matzah* into the pocket of a particularly handsome child to protect him/her against the evil eye.

xv. Since fish live beneath the water's surface and cannot be seen, they are, according to the Talmud *Berachot 20a,* immune from the effects of the evil eye. Therefore, putting them on an amulet ought to be quite effective!

xvi. The "fig" figure, a phallic symbol represented by the thumb thrust out between the first and second fingers, will work to avert the evil eye.

Counteractive Measures

i. "Whoever is afraid of the evil eye should stick his right thumb in his left hand and his left thumb in his right hand, proclaiming: 'I, so and so, son of so and so, am of the seed of Joseph, whom the evil eye may not affect'" (Talmud *Berachot 55b*).

ii. To divert the glance from the intended target, hang interesting objects (e.g. precious stones) between the eyes of the endangered person (*Tosef., Shabbat 4:5*).

iii. Qualify any praise that you give a beautiful object or person with the phrase *keyn ayen hore* ("may there be no evil eye"), often shortened to *kaynahora.*

8

Notable Angel Quotations and Stories

The following represent a cross section of what Jewish tradition has written and said about angels.

Chassidic and Kabbalistic Quotes

Chassidim often believed that angels were able to choose the kind of people they accompanied by observing their deeds. Deeds of mercy created merciful angels, while deeds of evil created bad angels.

1. Every *mitzvah* that a man does is not only an act of transformation in the material world; it is also a spiritual act, sacred in itself and this aspect of concentrated spirituality and holiness in the *mitzvah* is the chief component of that which becomes an angel (Adin Steinsaltz).

2. The virtue of angels is that they cannot deteriorate. Their flaw is that they are unable to improve. A human's flaw is that he can deteriorate, and a human's virtue is that he can improve (Chasidic saying).

Talmudic Quotes

There are many talmudic references to angels describing them in terms of when and how they were created, where they live, their missions, and how they are able to be maintained and stay alive.

1. In the world above, there is no sitting down and no competition. Angels do not have backs and experience no fatigue (Talmud *Chagigah 15a*).

2. One verse says, "Each of the angels had six wings" [Isa. 6:2], while another verse says, "And every one had four faces, and every one of them had four wings" [Ezek. 1:6]. There is no contradiction. The first verse speaks of the time when the Temple was still standing while the second verse is of the time when the Temple was no longer standing, when, if a person dare mention such a thing, the wings of the celestial creatures were diminished. Which wings were removed? Those with which they used to sing songs, said Rabbi Chananel in the name of Rav (Talmud *Chagigah 13b*).

3. It has been taught: Michael arrives with one flap of his wings, Gabriel with two, Elijah with four. The Angel of Death arrives with eight, but during a pestilence, he, too, arrives with only one flap of the wings (Talmud *Berachot 4b*).

4. Samuel said to Chiya bar Rav: O son of a lion of a man, come and I will let you know of some of the beautiful things that your father used to say: Each and every day ministering angels are created by the fire river, sing songs, and then no longer exist, as it is written, "because they are new every morning, the praise of Your faithfulness is great" [Lam. 3:23] (Talmud *Chagigah 14b*).

5. Rabbi Yochanan expressed the view that God does not rejoice in the downfall of evil people. The ministering angels wanted to sing hymns at the destruction of the

Egyptians, but God said "My children lie drowned in the sea, and you want to sing" (Talmud *Megillah 10b*)? [Note: To this day this passage influences Jewish liturgy. Only a half *Hallel* (Psalms of Praise), sometimes called the *Egyptian Hallel,* is recited during the intermediate days of Passover to temper the joy because of all the death that resulted from the Ten Plagues.]

6. The Rabbis teach: When Israel is in difficulty, and one among them separates himself, the two ministering angels who accompany a person lay their hands on his head, and say, "This person, who has separated himself from the community, shall not see its consolation." And it is taught: If the community is in difficulty, a person must not say, "I will go to my house and eat and drink, and peace shall be with you, O my soul." But a person must share in the trouble of the community. (Talmud *Taanit 11a*).

7. Our rabbis taught: There was a Sadducee who prepared the incense outside and brought it to the Holy of Holies. When leaving, his father said to him: "My son, even though we are Sadducees, we are not to prepare the incense outside for fear of the Pharisees." The son answered: "All of my days I have been agitated by the verse 'I appear in the cloud upon the Ark cover' [Leviticus 16:2], saying to myself: 'When shall the chance come my way for me to fulfill the precept? Now that it has come my way, should I not do it?'"

It is said: In a few days he died, his body was thrown on a dungheap, and worms came slithering out of his nose. Some say: 'He was killed as he came out of the Holy of Holies.' For Rabbi Chiya taught: Some kind of noise was heard in the Temple court because an angel came and struck him. He fell face down. When his brother priests came in, they found the imprint of something like a calf's foot on his shoulder. For of angels it is written, "Their feet were straight ones, and the sole of their feet was like the sole of a calf's foot" [Ezek. 1:7] (Talmud *Yoma 19b*).

8. Every day an angel goes out from the Presence of the Holy One to destroy the world and return it back to what it used to be. But once the Holy One observes young children in their schools and students of the wise in their house of study, God's anger immediately turns to kindness (*Ka R 2*).

9. Rabbi Chanina bar Papa taught: The name of the angel in charge of conception is Night. He takes a drop of semen and places it before the Holy One, saying to God: "Master of the Universe, what is this drop going to become, a strong or a weak person, a wise person or fool, a rich or poor person?" But he does not say, "A righteous person or a wicked person?" Rabbi Chanina added: "All is in the hands of heaven except the fear of Heaven, as it is written, 'And now, O Israel, what is the thing that God wants of you?' It is to fear Heaven" [Deut. 10:12] (Talmud *Niddah 16b*).

10. Rabbi Eliezer, son of Rabbi Yose the Galilean, said: "If you are aware of a righteous person about to go on a journey, and you intend to go in the same direction, start out as many as three days earlier or as many as three days later, so that you set out on the journey together with him, because the angels of peace accompany him, he being told, 'For God will give the angels charge over you, to keep you in all your ways'" [Ps. 91:11] (*Tosefta Avodah Zarah 1:17*).

11. Rabbi Yochanan said: "Righteous people are greater than ministering angels" (Talmud *Sanhedrin 92b*).

12. Rabbi Eliezer said: "When a righteous person dies, three companies of ministering angels go forth to meet him. One says: 'Let him come in peace;' Another says: 'Let him rest on his couch.' And another says: 'Each may walk in his uprightness'" [Isa. 57:2] (Talmud *Ketubot 104a*).

13. Rabbi Eliezer said: "Righteous souls are treasured under the Throne of Glory, as it is said, 'The soul of my lord

shall be cherished in the treasury of life' [1 Sam. 25:29]. But the wicked soul is tied up and tossed about. For one angel stands at one end of the world and another angel stands at the world's other end, and they sling the souls to each other, as it is said, 'The souls of your enemies, them shall God sling out, as from the hollow of a sling'" [1 Sam. 25:29] (Talmud *Shabbat 152b*).

14. Rabbi Simlai delivered the following lecture: "What does an embryo in its mother's womb look like? A ledger that stays folded up. The hands of the embryo rest on its two temples, its elbows on its two knees, and its heels against its buttocks. Its head lies between its knees, its mouth is closed, and its navel wide open. It eats what its mother eats and drinks what its mother drinks, but produces no waste, because otherwise it would kill its mother.

During the gestation period light burns above its head and as it gazes it can see from one end of the world to the other. There is no time during which a person is happier than in those days. At that time he is taught the entire Torah, all of it. But as he emerges into the air of the world, an angel appears, hits it in its mouth, and makes him forget the entire Torah" (Talmud *Sanhedrin 37b*).

15. Our rabbis taught: "Six things are said about human beings. In regard to three of them, they are like ministering angels, and in regard to three others, they are like animals. They are like ministering angels in these three ways: they have understanding like ministering angels, they walk erect like them and they use the sacred tongue like ministering angels" (Talmud *Chagigah 16a*).

16. Once, when Rabbi Joshua ben Chananiah and Rabbi Yose the Priest were strolling along the highway, they said: "Let us expound upon the work of the Chariot." Rabbi Joshua began his exposition. That particular day was the day of the summer solstice. Nevertheless, the heavens became cloudy and a kind of rainbow appeared in the cloud,

and the ministering angels assembled and came to listen, just like people who gather and come to watch the entertainment for bride and bridegroom. Later on Rabbi Yose the Priest went and related what had happened to Rabban Yochanan ben Zakkai, who said: "Happy are you, and happy is she that gave birth to you. Happy are my eyes that behold you who have seen such a sight. Moreover, in a dream I saw you and me reclining on Mount Sinai when a divine voice was sent to us from heaven saying, 'Ascend hither, ascend hither.' Here are great banqueting chambers and lovely couches spread out for you. You and your students and your students' students are designated for the third company of the upright" (Talmud *Chagigah 14b*).

17. When the wicked Nimrod threw our ancestor Abraham into the open fire, the angel Gabriel spoke up to the Holy One: "Master of the Universe, may I go down and cool the fire, to save the righteous man from burning in it?" The Holy One answered: "I am the unique one in My world, even as he is this unique one in his. It is appropriate that the Unique One deliver the unique one." But since the Holy One does not hold back the reward of any creature, he said to Gabriel, "Yours will be the privilege of saving three of his descendants" (Talmud *Pesachim 118a*).

18. Rabbi Simai taught: "When Israel hastened to say, 'We will do,' before saying, 'we will listen,' sixty myriads of ministering angels came down and fastened two crowns upon each and every one in Israel, one as a reward for saying 'we will do,' and the other as a reward for saying 'we will listen.' But when Israel transgressed, a hundred and twenty myriads of destructive angels came down and removed the crowns, as it is written, 'The children of Israel were stripped of their ornaments from Mount Horeb'" [Ex. 33:6] (Talmud *Shabbat 88a*).

19. True dreams come from angels—false dreams come from demons (adapted from Talmud *Berachot 55b*).

20. Those who pray in Aramaic will get no assistance from angels. They do not understand this language (Talmud *Shabbat 12b*).

Midrashic Quotes

Angel stories and quotations abound in the various rabbinic *midrashim*. Here is a cross-section of some of what has been said and written about angels over the centuries in the various *midrashim*.

1. The angels are kept alive only by the splendor of God's Presence, as it is said, "You keep them all alive, and the heavenly hosts bow before You" [Neh. 9:6] (*Midrash of Exodus Rabbah 32:4*).

2. We have been taught: "One angel is not capable of performing two missions simultaneously, nor do two angels perform a single mission together" (*Midrash of Genesis Rabbah 50:2*).

3. Four companies of ministering angels sing praise before the Holy Blessed One: the first camp, that of Michael; the second camp, that of Gabriel, at God's left; the third camp, that of Uriel, in front of God; and the fourth camp, that of Raphael behind God. God's Presence is thus in the center. God is seated on a lofty throne and exalted—high up and suspended above in space. The reflections of God's glory have an amber gleam. Upon God's head there is a crown, the diadem of the Explicit Name on the forehead. God's eyes range over the whole earth. Half of God's Presence is fire, the other half hail. At God's right is life, and at God's left, death. God holds a scepter of fire in His hand, and a veil is spread before God. Within the veil, the curtain, seven angels serve God. Under God's Throne of Glory is something like a sapphire. Fire continuously flashes around God's throne, and mercy and justice form the foundation of

it. Seven clouds of glory surround it, and a spinning wheel-angel, a cherub, and a celestial creature utter praises before God (*Pirke of Rabbi Eliezer, 4*).

4. Rabbi Ishmael said: "Metatron, the prince of the Presence, said to me: 'When the Holy Blessed One took me to serve under the Throne of Glory and under the wheel of the chariot and to all other appurtenances of the Divine Presence, my flesh turned into flaming fire, my sinews into glowing fire and my bones into coals of broom. My eyelids became like the brightness of the firmament, the spheres of the eye like fiery torches, the hairs of my head like a scorching fire. All of my body parts turned into pinions of fire, my whole body into blistering fire. At my right were piercing tongues of fire, at my left lit torches, and all about me a burgeoning whirlwind'" (*Hechalot*).

5. Rabbi Akiba said: "Each day in the morning an angel opens its mouth and says, 'God reigns, God did reign, and God will reign forever and ever,' until it reaches the words, 'Bless you.' When it reaches 'bless you,' a chariot creature stands up in the firmament whose name is Israel and upon whose brow the word 'Israel' is inscribed. Standing in the middle of the firmament, it says, 'Bless you God who should be blessed.' And all the celestial beings respond 'Blessed is God who should be blessed forever and forever.'

In the firmament there is one angelic creature upon whose brow is written the symbol "truth" when it is daytime, and this is how the angels know when it is day. In the evening, the word "faithfulness" is written on its brow and thus the angels know when it is nighttime. Each time it says 'Bless God who should be blessed,' the entire army of angels above respond: 'Blessed is God who should be blessed forever and ever'" (*Hechalot*).

6. Hadrian, may his bones be grounded into dust, asked Rabbi Joshua the son of Chananiah: "Do you maintain that there is no company of angels above who praise God and

repeat God's praise, but that every day the Holy Blessed One has to create a new company of angels who sing songs to God and then disappear?" Rabbi Joshua said: "Yes." Hadrian then asked: "Where do they go?" Rabbi Joshua responded: "To the place where they were created." Hadrian then asked: "Where were they created?" Rabbi Joshua answered: "In the fire river." Then Hadrian asked: "What is the nature of the fire river?" To which Rabbi Joshua answered: "It is like the Jordan River, which does not stop flowing either day or night." Hadrian then asked: "Where is its source?" Rabbi Joshua replied: "In the perspiration of the angels—the sweat from carrying the Throne of the Holy Blessed One" (*Midrash of Genesis Rabbah 78:1*).

7. On what day of the week were the angels created? Rabbi Yochanan said: "On day two of creation." Rabbi Chanina said: "On the fifth day."

Rabbi Luliani said in the name of Rabbi Isaac: "All agree that the angels were not created on the first day, so that it should not be said, 'While Michael was stretching out the firmament to the south, and Gabriel to the north, the Holy Blessed One was stretching out the firmament in the middle.' The fact of the matter is that God said: 'I am God that makes all things, that alone stretches the heaven above and the earth abroad by Myself' ("meitti") [Isa. 44:24]. 'Meitti,' 'by Myself' when read as 'mi itti'—who with Me, means: 'In the work of the creation of the world, who was partners with Me?'" (*Midrash of Genesis Rabbah 1:3*).

8. "God of differing manifestations of will" [Hos. 12:6]: God exercises upon the angels, when God wills it. When God desires it, God has them come into being seated. At times God wills it that they come into being standing. At other times God makes them in the likeness of women or of men, at times as winds and at times as fire. When by God's command they behave like messengers, they are made winds. When they minister before God, they are

made of fire, as it is written, "who makes winds Your messengers, fiery flames God's servants" (*Midrash of Exodus Rabbah 25:2*).

9. "God makes peace in the high places" [Job 25:2]. Michael is the prince of snow and Gabriel the prince of fire. Yet Michael does not extinguish Gabriel nor does Gabriel incinerate Michael. Even when half of an angel is fire and the other half is snow, the Holy Blessed One is able to make peace between the two parts (*Song of Songs Rabbah 3:11*).

10. "Go, get yourself down" [Ex. 32:7]. According to Rabbi Isaac, when the Holy One said to Moses, "Go, get yourself down," Moses' face grew dark. In the greatness of his distress, he became as one blind and thus did not know which way to go down. The ministering angels, saying "This is the time to kill him," were about to do just that. But the Holy One was aware of what they planned. And what did God do? It is said in the name of Rabbi Abba bar Aibu that the Holy One opened a wicket door under His throne of glory and said, "Go, get yourself down."

In the name of Rabbi Judah bar Ilai, it is said: "When Moses was about to get down, the angels came to kill him. What did he do? He took hold of the throne of the Holy One and the Holy One spread out the mantle over him, so that they would not harm him" (*Midrash of Exodus Rabbah 42:4*).

11. "And he called the name of that place Machanaim" [Gen. 32:3]. What is the meaning of "Machanaim?" Two camps. For when Jacob set out for Aram Naharaim, the guardian angels of the Land of Israel protected him and escorted him until he was out of the Land. Then these angels left, and other angels came to escort Jacob. When he returned from Laban, the angels who had been assigned to him continued to escort him as far as the Land of Israel. Once the guardian angels of the Land of Israel became aware that Jacob was coming, they went out of the Land to

join the escort, as it is said, "The angels of God met him before he crossed the Jordan" [Gen. 32:2]. Thus it happened that two camps of angels were standing along side Jacob—he sent messengers from both on the mission in his behalf (*Tanchuma, Vayishlach, 3*).

12. "And Jacob sent angels" [Gen. 32:4]. Jacob was given two camps of ministering angels. How many angels are in each camp of God? Two thousand myriads, for it is written, "God's mounted angels are twice a thousand myriads" [Ps. 68:18] (*Midrash of Genesis Rabbah 75:11*).

13. "Weeping she makes weep" [Lam. 1:2]. She weeps and makes the Holy One weep with her. She weeps and makes the ministering angels weep with her. She weeps and makes heaven and earth cry with her. She weeps and makes the hills and mountains cry with her (*Midrash of Lamentations Rabbah, 1:2*).

9

Notable Quotations Relating to the Angel of Death and Satan

Here is a cross-section of talmudic and midrashic quotations related to the Angel of Death, Satan, and evil spirits.

Angel of Death

1. Rabbi Chisda was sitting in Rav's school studying, so that the Angel of Death was not able to come near to him, for his mouth did not stop reciting the words of the lore. But when he proceeded to sit down on a cedar bench in the school, the Angel of Death made it split under him, so that Rabbi Chisda was silent for a moment. In that very moment [of silence], the Angel of Death took him (Talmud *Makkot 10a*).

2. While sitting at the bedside of Rabbi Nachman, Rava saw him falling toward the sleep of death, yet Rabbi Nach-

man managed to say to Rava, "Master, tell the Angel of Death not to torment me." Rava answered, "Master, are you not important that you cannot say it to him yourself?" Rav Nachman asked, "Who is sufficiently important and esteemed to make such a request?" Then Rava asked Rav Nachman, "Master, show yourself to me in a dream." When after his death he did show himself, Rava asked him, "Master, did you incur any pain?" He replied, "As little as pulling a hair out of milk. Yet, if the Holy One were to say to me, 'Go back to that world and become again what you once were,' I would not want it, the fear of the Angel of Death being so great" (Talmud *Moed Katan, 28a*).

3. The Angel of Death revealed itself to Rav Sheshet in the marketplace. Rav Sheshet said to him: "Will you capture me in the marketplace like cattle? Come to my house."

The Angel of Death appeared to Rav Ashi in the marketplace. Rav Ashi said to him, "Give me a thirty day break, so that I may review my studies, inasmuch as it is said, 'Happy is the one who comes here with learning in hand.'"

When the Angel of Death returned on the thirtieth day, Rav Ashi asked him: "What is the rush?" The Angel of Death replied, "Rav Huna bar Nathan is close on your heels, and remember, 'No sovereignty may infringe upon another even by as little as a hairbreadth'" (Talmud *Moed Katan 28a*).

4. Rabbi Joshua ben Levi said: "The Angel of Death told me three things: when dressing in the morning, do not take your shirt from your attendant, do not allow water to be poured over your hands by one who has not washed his hands, and do not stand in front of women when they are returning from the presence of a deceased person, because, sword in hand, I go leaping in front of them, and have permission to do harm. If one should happen to meet such women, what is the cure? He should remove himself a distance of four cubits. If there is a nearby river, let him

cross it. If there is another road, let him take it. If there is a wall, let him stand behind it. If he is unable to do any of these things, let him turn his face away and say, 'God said to Satan, "God rebuke you, O Satan,"' and so forth [Zech. 3:2] until they have passed by" (Talmud *Berachot 51a*).

Satan

1. When Noah began planting, Satan came by, and standing before him, asked, "What are you planting?" Noah answered, "A vineyard." Satan then asked: "What is its nature?" Noah answered: "Its fruit, fresh or dried, is sweet, and from it wine is fashioned that gladdens a person's heart."

Satan then asked, "Would you like the two of us to plant it together?" Noah answered, "Yes."

What did Satan do? He brought a ewe lamb and slaughtered it over the vine. Then he brought a lion, which he also killed over the vine. He brought a monkey, which he also killed over the vine, and finally a pig, which he slaughtered over the vine. With the blood that dripped from them, he watered the vineyard.

This escapade was Satan's way of saying that when a person drinks one cup of wine, he acts like a ewe lamb, with humility. When he drinks two, he becomes mighty as a lion and haughty, saying "who is like me?" When he drinks three or four cups of wine, he becomes like a monkey, hopping all about, dancing, laughing, saying obscene things in public, without realizing what he is doing. Finally, when he becomes totally intoxicated, he is like a pig, wallowing in mud and coming to rest among garbage (*Midrash of Tanchum Noah 13*).

2. Rabbi Chanina son of Rabbi Idi said: "The letter *samech* appears here for the first time in the Torah, which

implies that when Eve was created, Satan was created with her" (*Midrash of Genesis Rabbah 17:6*).

3. The rabbis in Rabbi Ishmael's school taught: "Until a young man reaches age twenty, the Holy One sits and waits expectantly, saying 'When will this man take a wife?' But when the young man reaches the age of twenty and has still not married, God says, 'May the bones of this one be blasted.'"

Rabbi Chisda said: "Why am I superior to my colleagues in learning? Because I was married at age sixteen. Had I gotten married at age fourteen, I would not have been able to say to Satan, 'An arrow in your eye'" (Talmud *Kiddushin 29b*).

4. Our rabbis taught: "Those who are occupied in eulogizing may, as long as the body is still before them, step aside one by one to recite the Shema prayer. When the body is no longer before them, they may sit down to recite it, while the mourner sits silently. When they stand up to recite the Tefillah, the mourner should rise to resign himself to God's judgment as he says, 'Master of the Universe, I have greatly transgressed before you, and You did not requite me even a thousandth part. O God, may it be Your desire that in compassion You heal the breaches that we have suffered and those suffered by all of your people Israel.'"

Abaye said: "A man should not speak this way, for we have been taught in the name of Rabbi Yose that a man should not provide an opening for Satan to make accusations" (Talmud *Berachot 14a*).

5. You will find that the numerical value of the letters in *hasatan* (i.e. Satan), the Adversary, is three hundred and sixty four, which is one short of the number of days in the year. Thus the Adversary is given the authority to accuse the Israelites on all days of the year except for the Day of

Atonement [Yom Kippur], for the Holy One said to him, "You have no authority to touch them."

Then, when the Adversary goes and finds all of them fasting and in prayer, dressed in white garments and clothed like the ministering angels, he immediately returns in shame and confusion. The Holy One asks him, "What have you discovered about My children?"

Satan answers, "They are like ministering angels, and I am unable to touch them." At once, the Holy One shackles the Adversary and announces to the Israelites, "I have forgiven you" (*Midrash of Psalms 27:4*).

6. The rabbis taught in the name of Rabbi Yose: "A person should never give Satan the opportunity to open his mouth" (Talmud *Berachot 60a*).

7. There were two men who were goaded by Satan, so that every Sabbath evening, just as the sun was going to set, they began to argue. Rabbi Meir happened to visit them and for three Sabbaths stopped them from quarreling, until peace was made between them. Then Rabbi Meir heard Satan cry out, "Woe. Rabbi Meir has thrown me out of my home" (Talmud *Gittin 52a*).

8. Rabbi Akiba used to mock sexual transgressors. Once Satan, disguised as a provocative woman, appeared to him on top of a palm tree. Akiba took hold of the tree and started to climb it. Reaching halfway, his evil impulse let go of him. Satan said to him, "Had it not been proclaimed of you in the firmament 'Take heed of Rabbi Akiba and his learning,' I would have valued your life at no more than two *meah*" (Talmud *Kiddushin 81a*).

9. Rabbi Joshua the son of Levi said: "After Moses had descended from God's Presence, Satan appeared and asked him bluntly, 'Master of the Universe, where is the Torah?' He answered, 'I gave it to the earth.' Satan then went to the earth and asked, 'Where is the Torah?' The earth re-

sponded, 'God understands the way thereof, and God knows the place' [Job 28:23]. Satan then went to the sea, which replied, 'It is not with me' [Job 28:14]. Finally, Satan went to the deep underneath the earth, which replied, 'It is not in me'" [Job 28:14].

So Satan returned to the Holy One and said: 'Master of the Universe, I searched for it everywhere in the world but did not find it.' God then said, 'Go to the son of Amram.' Satan went to Moses and asked, 'Where is the Torah that the Holy One gave to you?' Moses answered, 'Who am I that the Holy One should have given the Torah to me?' The Holy One asked, 'Moses, are you a liar?' Moses replied, 'Master of the Universe, You had hidden away a precious thing in which You delighted every day. Shall I now claim credit for myself for it?' The Holy One said to Moses: 'Since you make so little of yourself, the Torah shall be called by Your name—remember you the Torah of Moses My servant'" [Mal. 3:22] (Talmud *Shabbat 89a*).

10. Rabbi Shimon said in the name of Rabbi Joshua: "Why does the *kohen gadol* not enter the Holy of Holies dressed in golden garments? Because whatever invites accusation should not be in sight when defense is required, in order that Satan not be given a chance to say in accusation, 'Only yesterday these people made themselves a god of gold and today they have the audacity to serve God in golden garments'" (*Midrash of Leviticus Rabbah 21:10*).

11. The rabbis taught that Satan, the Angel of Death, and the evil impulse are one (Talmud *Baba Batra 16a*).

12. Satan seduces us in this world and accuses in the next (Talmud *Sukkah 52b*).

13. Satan's torment is worse than that of Job. He was like a servant told to break a cask without spilling the wine (Talmud *Baba Batra 16b*).

14. Like iron, out of which a person can fashion whatever tools one needs when one heats it in the forge, so Satan can be subdued to the service of God, if tempered by the fiery Torah (*Avot de Rabbi Nathan 16*).

15. It is difficult for Satan alone to mislead the world, so he appointed rabbis in different places (Rabbi Nachman of Bratslav).

16. You cannot trust Satan. He tries to persuade you not to go to the synagogue on a cold morning and when you do go, he follows you there (Koretser Rabbi).

17. The evil impulse is known by many names: snake, crooked one, Satan, Angel of Death, unclean one, enemy, stumbling stone, uncircumcised, evil one and the northern *tzeefonee* (*Zohar ii, 182a*).

18. When does Satan turn informer? When his victim turns away from him to repentance (*Zohar Chadash i, 20a*).

10

Who's Who of Angels and Demons

The following is a summary of some of the most well known and often quoted angels and demons in Jewish and the Ancient Near Eastern tradition.

Agrat bat Machlat Dancing roof demon.

Azazel Demon thought to live in the wilderness.

Asmodeus (destroyer) A destructive angel who was considered the king of all of the demons (Psalm 11).

Baradiel The angel of hail.

Barakiel Angel in charge of lightning.

Beelzebub (lord of the flies) The sovereign of the netherworld.

Belial Another title for Satan, frequently identified as the spirit of evil in the Dead Sea Scrolls.

Cherubim Beings whose purpose was to guard the Tree of Life in the Garden of Eden (Gen. 3:24). They were also portrayed on the Ark of the Covenant.

Dever Demon of pestilence.

Dybbuk A clinging soul that enters a person's body and speaks through his mouth. Very menacing ones require the rite of exorcism.

Fallen Angel   A vanquished demon who appears as accursed.

Gabriel   One of the two angels mentioned by name in the Bible (Dan. 8:16). He was the leader of the archangels.

Galgalliel   Angel in charge of the sun's orb.

Jeqon   Fallen angel blamed for the downfall of angels.

Jeremiel   Angel in charge of seeds of netherworld.

Kategor   (accuser) Angel whose function it was to call attention to the transgressions of the people (Zech. 3:1).

Kesilim   Fooling spirits who misguide people and poke fun at them.

Ketev Meriri   Demon that is especially active during the morning.

Kokabriel   Angel in charge of stars.

Lailiel   Angel in charge of night.

Lilith   A female demon who reigned in the night (Isa. 34:14). In Jewish mysticism she is considered the queen of the demons.

Malach HaMavet   (Angel of Death) Angel whose purpose it was to summon the dying soul from the earth.

Mazzikim   Harmful spirits, said to have been created on the eve of the Sabbath of creation.

Matariel   Angel in charge of precipitation.

Metatron   In mystical literature, the highest celestial figure in the angelic world, sometimes known as the Angel of the Presence.

Michael   He was one of two angels mentioned by name in the Bible (Dan. 10:13).

Ophanim   (wheels) Appearing in the Book of Ezekiel, angels that dress the holy chariot.

Ra'amiel   Angel in charge of thunder.

Ra'asiel   Angel in charge of earthquakes.

Raguel   Angel who takes revenge on world of lights.

Raphael   (God heals) One of the seven archangels who brought prayers before God.

Resheph   The plague demon.

Rishpe   Demons living in the roots of trees.

Ruziel   (secret of God) The angel of magic.

Sandalfon   Name of one of the most exalted angels, having as his place an area behind the Heavenly Chariot of God.

Samael   The prince of the evil demons, often associated with Lilith, Satan and the Angel of Death.

Sanegor   (defender) An angel who defended the people in the heavenly court.

Satan   (adversary) One of his primary tasks was to call God's attention to the sins of the people.

Se'irim   Hairy demons.

Seraphim   (fiery angels) In Isaiah 6:2, angels described declaring God's holiness.

Shabriri   Demon causing blindness.

Shalgiel   Angel in charge of snow.

Shedim   Various kinds of demons appearing in talmudic literature.

Uriel   An angel classified as the prince of the archangels, and identified by thunder and earthquakes. He warned the people about the end of the world.

Za'amiel   Angel in charge of whirlwinds.

Za'apiel   Angel in charge of hurricanes.

FURTHER READING

Arzt, Max. *Justice and Mercy: Commentary on the Liturgy of the New Year and the Day of Atonement.* New York: Holt, Rinehart and Winston, 1963.

Bamberger, Bernard. *Fallen Angels.* Philadelphia: Jewish Publication Society, 1952.

Davidson, G. A. *A Dictionary of Angels.* New York: Free Press, 1967.

Ganzfried, Solomon. *Code of Jewish Law.* New York: Hebrew Publishing Company, 1961.

Gaster, T. H. *The Dead Sea Scriptures.* New York: Doubleday and Company, 1956.

Goodspeed, E. J. *The Apocrypha.* New York: Random House, 1959.

Scholem, Gershom. *Kabbalah.* Jerusalem: Keter Publishing House, 1974.

Steinsaltz, Adin. *The Thirteen Petalled Rose.* Northvale, N. J.: Jason Aronson, 1992.

Trachtenberg, Joshua. *Jewish Magic and Superstition: A Study in Folk Religion.* New York: Atheneum, 1975.

———. *The Devil and the Jews.* Philadelphia: Jewish Publication Society, 1961.

INDEX

About the Author

Rabbi Ronald Isaacs is the rabbi of Temple Sholom in Bridgewater New Jersey. He received his doctorate in instructional technology from Columbia University's Teacher's College. He is the author of numerous books, including *Loving Companions: Our Jewish Wedding Album,* coauthored with Leora Isaacs; *Words for the Soul: Jewish Wisdom for Life's Journey, Mitzvot: A Sourcebook for the 613 Commandments, Close Encounters,* and *The Jewish Book of Numbers.* Rabbi Isaacs is currently on the Publications Committee of both the Rabinical Assembly and C.A.J.E. and also serves on the editorial board of *Shofar Magazine.* He resides in Jew Jersey with his wife, Leora, and their children Keren and Zachary.